ALL DAY CAFE

ALL DAY CAFE

CAFE-STYLE FOOD TO MAKE AT HOME

STUART McKENZIE

MURDOCH BOOKS
SYDNEY · LONDON

CONTENTS

THE ROAD TO SOUTH OF JOHNSTON

~~~

Sharing, creativity, food, friends and socialising – I definitely chose the right industry! I was shy and lacking in confidence as a teenager, but hospitality work brought me out of my shell.

I always wanted to be an architect. As a child in suburban Melbourne, I was obsessed with Lego and empty cardboard boxes, thinking that was going to be my career path. One of the pivotal moments of my life was two weeks' work experience in an architectural practice. Best decision ever: knocked that idea right out of me.

During my last two years of school I worked almost every Saturday night at an artists' colony known as Montsalvat, for the formidable Sigmund Jorgensen. They held weddings and functions in the 1930s French chateau-style buildings – there was a very bohemian vibe and the hosts showed great flair at setting rooms with flowers, candles, silverware and crockery. Sigmund served sherry in antique mismatched glasses on the terrace, the sumptuous dinner buffet was covered in hand-picked edible flowers, tables were laid with rustic natural linens, and herbs from the farm were on display. It taught me great styling tips and the importance of being a generous host.

When I turned 17, I finished school and moved out of home and into the hip streets of inner-city Fitzroy. I landed a job at a heritage-listed pub that was rocking with live music and a bustling kitchen. We were overworked and underpaid but I loved it. The manager only ever called me James, after James Dean, because of my quiff. I learnt rostering and stock control, how to serve drinks and deal with inebriated punters. And this was my first opportunity to cook professionally.

My childhood hadn't been particularly culinary. Dad never cooked and my mother, Moira, had some standard meals that were well practised and delicious, but it's fair to say my childhood mealtimes were not gastronomic mind-blowing experiences. When my brother Paul began an apprenticeship as a chef, suddenly we were eating pasta with amazing sauces, chicken stuffed with pine nuts and chocolate coffee cake. When Paul moved out of home, he abandoned us again to toasted sandwiches, curried sausages and lamb chops. This forced me to experiment and the seed was sown.

Years later, when I was living on minimum wage in a shared house, creating meals was easier because of this experience. We shopped at markets and checked out specials, grew our own herbs and managed to host great dinner parties on the tightest of budgets. This passion for living well, but within my means, also followed through to the way I arranged my home. I started to collect furniture from vintage shops and council clean-ups, then painted, sanded, collated and arranged it. My eclectic style was evolving.

I worked my way through café and restaurant jobs, ranging in roles and responsibilities, and from Melbourne to Queensland's Port Douglas. In the mid-1990s, I was back in Melbourne, helping manage the popular Blue Train café. The owners of this incredibly busy business – Angela Mathioudakis, Paul Mathis and George Incretolli – taught me much about the industry. Their seemingly overnight success in this location (people would wait up to three hours for a table) didn't deter them from being very accessible, humble and grounded. I decided my destiny was to open my own café. Working predominantly during the daytime was a big plus and I felt it would suit my personality, being generally less formal than a restaurant environment.

In 2004 some friends from Blue Train café and I stumbled across a boarded-up former train station in Melbourne's Middle Park. We began refurbishing the space on a very small budget,

took out a few walls and built a fantastic wrap-around deck overlooking Albert Park. Mart 130 opened for business. Mart is Tram backwards, and 130 refers to the tram stop.

We kept the menu simple and created some great versions of breakfast and brunch classics. Sometimes it was trial and error, especially as the space was so small to cook in – part of the charm of Mart 130 was that we constantly changed the menu and styling of the space. We were very hands-on in our business, which the customers liked, and were open until 2011.

I had been commuting from Fitzroy for five years and wanted to work closer to home. There were already many cafés in the area, but I couldn't help thinking there was room for just one more. I found the perfect spot in Collingwood and managed to secure the lease of an old factory building at 46 Oxford Street. South of Johnston opened on Friday 13 April, 2012.

The space was much bigger: about three times the size of Mart 130. It required more thought to fit out and work in – the more space there is, the harder it is to delineate areas and make it feel cosy. With large warehouse spaces with 5-metre (16-foot) high industrial ceilings, it is important to get it right – from acoustics to heating, cooling, insulation and flow, to ambience in general.

It was when SoJo opened that I began thinking more about sustainability. I wanted to reduce waste, use ethically sourced ingredients and products, and save energy in the café. So all cardboard and plastic is recycled and the kitchen has organised for green waste to go to a family-run chook farm. I use suppliers within a certain radius of the café to reduce food miles. All our meat, poultry, fruit and vegetables, with a few exceptions, are from Victoria.

We insulated and lined the warehouse with timber. The skylights mean we are able to reduce the number of lights on during the day. And double glazing the skylights and all the windows has helped with heating and cooling. Little things, such as replacing all the overhead halogen lights for LED low voltage, helped but the biggest change was when we financed 40 solar panels on our roof – these generate about 60 per cent of our electricity.

We planted an orchard and herb garden in front of SoJo for our kitchen and local residents to use. Collingwood, as an inner-city neighbourhood, doesn't have a lot of green space, so this was not only practical, but also softens the edges of our harsh 1960s building and started to attract birds and bees. Now people refer to SoJo as 'the café with the planter boxes out the front', which I love.

At SoJo I was really keen to cook again. I find even the style of serving and the choosing of the crockery exciting parts of the whole process. Because we have a corporate lunchtime crowd from Monday to Friday, we can create more main meals, pastas and complex salads than I had served previously. Breakfast was always very popular, especially at weekends, but the new clientele, more room and dedicated staff have allowed us to get more creative.

Slower cooking, traditional methods, sourcing new ingredients, using seasonal produce and talking to our suppliers, keeping an eye on current food and drink trends, weighing up what sells and what doesn't, getting a liquor licence – it all adds to the excitement of experimentation that drives us forward.

Sometimes, though, people just want poached eggs and bacon. On toast. Gluten-free toast. And that's OK: it's what we do. But we make the eggs free-range, choose a fantastic loaf of bread from a local supplier, use the best organic bacon, cook it all really well and get them coming back (perhaps to experiment a little more next time).

01

SPRING

SPRING: CRISP MORNINGS AND BRIGHT SKIES TO INTRODUCE EACH DAY, EVEN IN THE INNER CITY

After the chill and darkness of winter, I start to wake up earlier in spring. Everything feels lighter and the world around me seems to flourish with new colour and life.

When we are creating the spring menu, the chefs and I always look at what is available at the markets and from local growers — easily available usually means the produce is more reasonably priced too. There are some favourite dishes that we keep on the menu all year round, but we also ensure there are lots of exciting seasonal changes, so our regular customers can appreciate the changing year.

Being in the city, we don't have vast landscapes unfolding in front of our eyes to herald the new spring growth. Not in Collingwood anyway! So, as part of creating a new menu, we also try to evoke what spring feels like and means to us, by using visual clues around the café. We pack away all the winter foliage, heavy colours and warm throws and reset the space with fresh, pastel-coloured flowers, bunches of colourful spring bulbs, big baskets of eggs and spring produce. The atmosphere is light, bright and fresh.

MIMOSAS

Serves 8

750 ml (26 fl oz) bottle
   good-quality Prosecco
375 ml (13 fl oz/1½ cups) freshly
   squeezed orange juice

For our mimosas we use a ratio of two parts Prosecco to one part orange juice, but you could make them with equal parts, so no one needs to worry about getting too plastered at brunch!

~~~~~~~~~~~~~~~~~~~~~

Keep both ingredients well chilled until ready to serve. Fill each champagne glass two-thirds full with the Prosecco, then top up with orange juice.

BANANA PASSIONFRUIT SMOOTHIE

Serves 2

1 banana
6 ice cubes
150 g (5½ oz) plain yoghurt
pulp of 1 passionfruit
½ vanilla bean, split in half
   lengthways, seeds scraped
500 ml (17 fl oz/2 cups) milk
1 tablespoon honey

This is a really tasty, healthy drink that's full of fibre and can be whipped up in minutes. It's the perfect snack to tide you over between meals and is good for energy replacement after sport. We sell a lot of these to people who don't enjoy coffee or tea, but still want a drink that they can take away in the morning along with everyone else.

~~~~~~~~~~~~~~~~~~~~~

Peel the banana, break it into 2.5 cm (1 inch) pieces and put in a blender. Add the ice cubes (see Cook's tips), yoghurt, passionfruit, vanilla seeds and milk.

Add the honey, making sure you drizzle it into the middle of the blender, so it is worked into the drink rather than getting stuck on the side of the jug.

Blend for 30 seconds, or until smooth and thick. Pour into two chilled glasses.

COOK'S TIPS

● *Make sure your blender is suitable for crushing ice. Blenders with plastic jugs are not durable enough for this – the ice can cause the plastic to become brittle and crack.*
● *If you have a low-powered blender, break up the ice cubes first: wrap them in a tea towel and smash on a hard surface.*

BERRY AND BANANA SALAD

Serves 4

125 g (4½ oz/1 punnet) blueberries
500 g (1 lb 2 oz/2 cups) plain
     yoghurt
2 tablespoons honey
200 g (7 oz/2 heaped cups) flaked
     almonds
125 g (4½ oz/½ punnet)
     strawberries, hulled and cut into
     quarters
125 g (4½ oz/½ punnet) raspberries
125 g (4½ oz/½ punnet) blackberries
2 bananas

This breakfast salad is a great way to appreciate the fantastic berries that are available in spring. Berries are loaded with antioxidants and vitamins and their incredible colours can be highlighted by serving in bowls of contrasting colours, or on patterned or vintage plates.

In a mixing bowl, lightly crush the blueberries with a fork, then add the yoghurt and honey. Stir well and refrigerate for 1 hour.

Heat a frying pan over medium heat. When the pan is hot, add the almonds and stir constantly until golden brown. Tip out onto paper towel to cool down and crisp up.

Put the remaining berries in a large mixing bowl. Peel the bananas and slice diagonally. Add to the berries and gently fold everything together.

Spoon the berry salad onto four plates. Top with a generous dollop of blueberry yoghurt and sprinkle with the toasted almonds.

BIRCHER MUESLI

Serves 4

Bircher muesli

190 g (6¾ oz/2 cups) rolled
   (porridge) oats
40 g (1½ oz/¼ cup) hazelnuts
40 g (1½ oz/¼ cup) sultanas
   (golden raisins)
125 g (4½ oz/½ cup) plain yoghurt
375 ml (13 fl oz/1½ cups) milk
60 ml (2 fl oz/¼ cup) fresh
   orange juice
60 ml (2 fl oz/¼ cup) thin
   (pouring) cream
60 ml (2 fl oz/¼ cup) honey
1 apple
1 orange

1 mango
2 passionfruit
125 g (4½ oz/1 punnet) blueberries
Granola, to serve (optional)
   (page 78)

Mix the muesli the night before and leave in the fridge to allow the oats to swell, the sultanas to plump up and all the other flavours to mingle. You can serve this with any fruit: choose what's fresh and in season.

TO MAKE THE BIRCHER MUESLI, combine the oats, hazelnuts and sultanas in a 2 litre (70 fl oz/8 cup) container. Stir in the yoghurt, milk, orange juice, cream and honey. Grate the apple, peel and dice the orange and add both to the muesli. Stir, then cover and refrigerate overnight.

To serve, slice the mango into wedges and cut each passionfruit in half. Place a cupful of bircher muesli in each bowl. Top with the mango wedges, blueberries and passionfruit pulp. If you like, you can sprinkle with some granola for a little extra crunch. Any left-over bircher muesli can be stored in the fridge for up to 3 days.

FLOWERS

~~~

While I like to buy a bunch or two of flowers for home most weeks, they are definitely a 'must have', rather than a luxury, at the café. Customers have come to expect and appreciate them. Flowers are an important decorative detail that can be easily and often changed without having to spend a lot of money. I prefer to buy varieties that are in season, rather than those reared in hot-houses, but it isn't always possible.

You don't always need to use flowers to make a statement either. Sometimes, when I come back from country Daylesford, I bring in bunches of lavender, bay leaves, rosemary, lemon thyme, oak and olive branches, gum nuts... foliage and herbs can work just as well as blooms.

As well as creating floral displays on the bar and in the hallway at SoJo, we also keep bunches in the bathrooms (especially the perfumed flowers, as I don't like to mix heavily scented flowers – or candles, for that matter – with food).

We put a few arrangements on the tabletops occasionally. The key is to keep these simple, using only one or two varieties of flower but in abundance. Just keep the water clean and make sure there's enough width and weight to the vase, jug or jar, so that it won't fall over easily. Also, keep the flower display relatively low, so it doesn't compete with the eyeline of conversation and so it won't get knocked over by gesticulating hands.

I collect small, colourful and inexpensive glass vases. Mismatched ones, which you can find at garage sales or junk shops for just a couple of dollars, look great when grouped together and filled with plain white orchid stems. Another idea, if you have a small budget, is to get some laboratory-style glass beakers and specimen jars. Once again, in a cluster, these can look fantastic, each holding just a single botanical stem, branch, leaf or whatever you fancy.

MARINATED FETA

Makes 500 g (1 lb 2 oz)

1 small handful of thyme sprigs
1 small handful of rosemary sprigs
4 bay leaves
12 peppercorns
¼ teaspoon chilli flakes (optional)
2 garlic cloves, thinly sliced
500 g (1 lb 2 oz) feta cheese, cut
    into 2 cm (¾ inch) cubes
olive oil, to cover

Marinated feta can be used in so many meals. Recently I've been using it with pasta dishes as an alternative to parmesan. It is also delicious on fresh crusty bread with slices of seasoned ripe tomato.

~~~~~~~~~~~~~~~~~~~~~~~

You will need to find a glass jar large enough to hold all the ingredients snuggly. Sterilise the jar and lid before use.

Place about a third of the herbs and spices in the bottom of the jar. Arrange half the cubed feta on top. Add another third of the herbs and spices, then the remaining feta. Finish with the remaining herbs and spices.

Cover with olive oil, then seal and refrigerate. The marinated feta will keep in the fridge for up to 1 month.

CRUSHED AVOCADO WITH FETA AND TOMATO

Serves 4

1 lemon
2 firm, ripe avocados
8 slices of the best sourdough you
  can find
butter, for the toast
4 vine-ripened tomatoes, sliced
100 g (3½ oz) Marinated feta,
  crumbled (recipe left)
1 small handful of basil leaves
1 small handful of flat-leaf (Italian)
  parsley leaves
extra virgin olive oil, for drizzling

Crushed avocado has become a staple in Melbourne's café culture over the past few years, so we daren't take it off the menu. It does, however, appear in various guises, depending on the season. Often, the simplest dishes that highlight produce at its freshest are the most enjoyable.

~~~~~~~~~~~~~~~~~~~~~~~~~~~

Cut the lemon in half. Slice one lemon half into wedges and set aside. Cut the avocados in half, remove the stones and then use a spoon to scoop the flesh into a small mixing bowl. Add the juice from the remaining lemon half, and season with sea salt and freshly ground pepper. Use a fork to crush everything together and set aside.

Toast the sourdough and spread with a little butter. Top each piece of toast with some sliced tomato, crushed avocado and feta.

Arrange on four serving plates. Tear the basil and parsley leaves and sprinkle over the top. Drizzle with a little extra virgin olive oil and serve with a wedge of lemon.

FRENCH TOAST WITH BALSAMIC STRAWBERRIES AND MACADAMIA CRUMBLE

Serves 4

Macadamia crumble

35 g (1¼ oz/¼ cup) plain
    (all-purpose) flour
2 tablespoons caster (superfine)
    sugar
50 g (1¾ oz) chilled unsalted butter,
    chopped
40 g (1½ oz/½ cup) shredded
    coconut
40 g (1½ oz/¼ cup) crushed
    macadamia nuts

Balsamic strawberries

55 g (2 oz/¼ cup) caster
    (superfine) sugar
1 tablespoon balsamic vinegar
300 g (10½ oz) strawberries, hulled

French toast

4 free-range eggs
80 ml (2½ fl oz/⅓ cup) milk
80 ml (2½ fl oz/⅓ cup) thin
    (pouring) cream
30 g (1 oz) unsalted butter
1 brioche loaf, about 400 g (14 oz),
    cut into 8 slices about 2 cm
    (¾ inch) thick

I'd recommend you start this recipe the day before, so your crumble and strawberries are ready to go, and all that needs to be done in the morning is to cook the French toast. At the café we often serve this with ice cream, even for breakfast, so look for the best vanilla ice cream you can find or have a go at making some yourself (page 122). Alternatively, serve with vanilla yoghurt or mascarpone.

~~~~~~~~

TO MAKE THE MACADAMIA CRUMBLE, preheat the oven to 180°C (350°F). Put the flour and sugar in a bowl and stir to combine. Add the butter and use your fingertips to rub the butter into the flour mixture. Stir in the coconut and macadamias.

Spread on a baking tray and bake for 20 minutes, or until the crumble is golden and crisp. Remove from the oven and allow to cool. The crumble can be stored in an airtight container for up to 1 week.

TO MAKE THE BALSAMIC STRAWBERRIES, put the sugar, balsamic vinegar and 2 tablespoons cold water in a small saucepan. Stir over low heat until the sugar has dissolved. Add the strawberries and increase the heat to high. Bring to the boil and cook for 3 minutes. Set aside to cool, then refrigerate until needed.

TO MAKE THE FRENCH TOAST, whisk together the eggs, milk and cream in a wide bowl. Melt half the butter in a large non-stick frying pan over medium heat. Dip four slices of bread, one at a time, in the egg mixture until soaked, then drain off the excess.

Fry the bread for 2 minutes on each side, or until golden brown. Remove from the pan and keep warm while you cook the remainder of the slices. Serve topped with the strawberries and crumble.

EGGS

For the best results, always use fresh, free-range eggs. We use a lot of eggs in our cooking and have built up a fabulous relationship with our supplier over the years. Always keep eggs in the fridge but take them out and let them come to room temperature before cooking. Here are some of our favourite egg recipes:

FRIED

Serves 4

80 ml (2½ fl oz/⅓ cup) olive oil
20 g (¾ oz) butter
8 free-range eggs

Heat half the olive oil and half the butter in a large non-stick frying pan over high heat.

Crack an egg into a saucer, then slide the egg into the pan. (Depending on the size of your pan, you could fry 4 eggs together.) Cook until the whites are opaque and the edges crisp. To help cook the yolks, spoon a little oil from the pan over the eggs.

For sunny-side down, use a spatula to carefully turn the eggs. Cook for a further 30 seconds if you like your egg yolk runny, or for 1 minute for a set yolk. Repeat with the remaining oil, butter and eggs.

SCRAMBLED

Serves 4

8 free-range eggs
80 ml (2½ fl oz/⅓ cup) thin (pouring) cream
50 g (1¾ oz) butter

Whisk the eggs and cream together in a bowl. Season with sea salt and freshly ground pepper.

Heat a heavy-based, non-stick frying pan over medium heat. Add the butter and, when it begins to sizzle, pour the egg mixture into the pan. Don't stir until the first signs of setting.

When the egg starts to set, stir gently using a wooden spoon or spatula to push the cooked egg towards the centre of the pan, tilting the pan to allow the uncooked egg to touch the base. Cook for 2 minutes, or until the eggs are just set. Remove from the heat and serve immediately.

POACHED

Serves 4

1 tablespoon vinegar
1 teaspoon sea salt
8 free-range eggs

● *Make sure your eggs are really fresh for poaching.*
● *Cracking the egg into a saucer first lets you check the yolk is intact and gives you better control when sliding it into the pan.*
● *While the eggs are cooking, and between each serve, use a slotted spoon to skim any foam off the water.*

Fill a wide saucepan or deep frying pan with water until about 10 cm (4 inches) deep. Add the vinegar and salt. Bring to the boil over medium–high heat, then reduce the heat so the water is just simmering.

Working with one egg at a time, crack the egg into a saucer or cup. Using a slotted spoon, stir the simmering water in one direction to create a whirlpool. Holding the saucer as close to the water as possible, gently slide the egg into the centre of the whirlpool. Repeat with the second egg.

Cook for 2–3 minutes for a soft yolk or 3–4 minutes for firm. Remove the eggs with the slotted spoon and drain on a plate lined with paper towel. Repeat with the remaining eggs and serve everyone two eggs each with some toast.

OMELETTE

Serves 1

3 free-range eggs
1½ tablespoons thin (pouring) cream
20 g (¾ oz) butter

Filling suggestions
leg ham, roasted tomato and bocconcini (fresh baby mozzarella cheese)
zucchini (courgette), asparagus and goat's cheese

Preheat the oven to 180°C (350°F). Whisk the eggs and cream together and season with sea salt and freshly ground pepper.

Melt the butter in an ovenproof, non-stick frying pan over medium heat. Pour the egg into the pan, but don't stir until the first signs of setting. Then, gently stir using a wooden spoon or spatula to push the cooked egg towards the centre of the pan, tilting the pan to allow the uncooked egg to touch the base. As soon as the egg starts to set, scatter your chosen filling over half the omelette.

Place the pan in the oven and cook for a further 3 minutes, or until just cooked through. Use a spatula to fold the omelette in half, then serve.

SALMON EGGS WITH RED ONION AND DILL SALSA

Serves 4

Red onion and dill salsa

½ small red onion, finely diced

2 tablespoons capers

1 small handful of dill, finely chopped

extra virgin olive oil

lemon juice

---

8 free-range eggs

8 slices of sourdough

250 g (9 oz/1 cup) crème fraîche (see Cook's tips)

2 handfuls of baby English spinach leaves

8 slices of good-quality smoked salmon or gravlax

COOK'S TIPS

Ricotta cheese can be used as a low-fat substitute for the crème fraîche.

Another perennial café favourite is the combination of smoked salmon and eggs, served here with a red onion salsa. I love the juxtaposition of the velvety crème fraîche with the bite of the salsa, the earthiness of the spinach and the warm, golden egg yolks on crunchy toast.

TO MAKE THE RED ONION AND DILL SALSA, combine the onion, capers and dill in a bowl. Drizzle with extra virgin olive oil, squeeze in some lemon juice and season to taste with sea salt and freshly ground pepper. Set aside for up to 2 hours.

Poach the eggs for 2–4 minutes in a pan of simmering water (page 33).

Meanwhile, toast the sourdough and spread with crème fraîche. Arrange the toast on four plates. Top with baby spinach, a slice of smoked salmon and the poached eggs. Finish with a generous tablespoon of the salsa.

GREEN EGGS

Serves 4

16 asparagus spears
8 free-range eggs
80 ml (2½ fl oz/⅓ cup) thin
    (pouring) cream
50 g (1¾ oz) butter
4 tablespoons Pesto (page 88)
100 g (3½ oz) goat's cheese
    (see Cook's tips)
8 slices of sourdough
butter, for the toast
smoked salmon or fried bacon
    (optional)
torn basil and/or parsley leaves,
    to garnish

COOK'S TIPS

Instead of goat's cheese, you could use ricotta, marinated feta, parmesan or gruyère.

The perfect springtime breakfast can be made even better by adding smoked salmon or bacon. If you can't get asparagus, wilted spinach makes a great substitute.

To blanch the asparagus, bring a saucepan of water to the boil. Snap off and discard the woody ends from the asparagus, add to the boiling water and blanch for 1 minute. Refresh in a bowl of iced water, then drain.

Whisk the eggs and cream in a bowl and season with sea salt and freshly ground pepper.

Heat the butter in a heavy-based, non-stick frying pan over medium heat. Add the egg mixture, then when the egg starts to set, add the pesto and goat's cheese. Using a wooden spoon or spatula, gently stir the pesto and cheese through the eggs. Push the cooked egg towards the centre of the pan, tilting the pan to allow the uncooked egg to touch the base. Cook for 2 minutes, or until the eggs are just set.

Meanwhile, toast the sourdough and spread with a little butter. Place two slices of toast on each plate and top with the scrambled eggs and asparagus. Add some smoked salmon or fried bacon, if desired. Garnish with torn basil and parsley.

CRUSHED PEAS, EGGS AND PROSCIUTTO

Serves 4

Crushed peas

85 ml (2¾ fl oz) extra virgin
   olive oil
1 small onion, finely diced
600 g (1 lb 5 oz) fresh shelled peas
   or thawed frozen peas
2 tablespoons finely chopped
   oregano
2 tablespoons finely chopped mint
1 teaspoon finely chopped
   preserved lemon rind (page 56)

8 free-range eggs
8 slices of sourdough or rye bread
butter, for the toast
8 slices of good-quality prosciutto
   or pancetta
Slow-roasted roma (plum)
   tomatoes (page 93)
200 g (7 oz) fresh ricotta cheese,
   crumbled
pea shoots or torn parsley leaves,
   to garnish.

The combination of crushed peas, sweet tomatoes, creamy ricotta and salty prosciutto is a match made in breakfast heaven. The addition of poached eggs turns this into pure breakfast indulgence.

TO MAKE THE CRUSHED PEAS, heat 1 tablespoon of the olive oil in a saucepan over medium heat. Add the onion and sauté for about 5 minutes, or until soft. Add the peas, chopped herbs and preserved lemon. Season with a good pinch of sea salt and freshly ground pepper. Cover with the lid and cook the peas for 4 minutes.

Using a potato masher, crush the peas in the pan, making sure you retain some texture – this is not a purée! Stir in the remaining oil and adjust the seasoning if necessary. This can be prepared up to a day in advance and stored, covered, in the fridge.

Poach the eggs for 2–4 minutes in a pan of simmering water (page 33).

Toast the sourdough, then spread with a little butter and a generous amount of crushed peas. Top with the prosciutto, roasted tomatoes, some crumbled ricotta and a poached egg. Garnish with pea shoots.

THAI-STYLE PUMPKIN AND COCONUT SOUP

Serves 4–6

1 tablespoon olive oil

1 onion, diced

3 garlic cloves, minced

2 bird's eye chillies, sliced

1 cm (½ inch) piece of fresh ginger, peeled and sliced

1 cm (½ inch) piece of galangal, peeled and sliced

1 lemongrass stem, pale part only, sliced

2 kaffir lime leaves, sliced

3 coriander (cilantro) roots, washed and crushed

2 x 420 g (15 oz) tins coconut cream

1 kg (2 lb 4 oz) butternut pumpkin (squash), peeled and cut into chunks (see Cook's tips)

1.5 litres (52 fl oz/6 cups) Vegetable stock (page 151)

1 tablespoon fish sauce, or to taste (optional)

bean sprouts, coriander (cilantro) leaves, Vietnamese mint and lime wedges, to serve

Here, the classic pumpkin soup is taken to new heights with some spicy Thai flavours. The coconut milk gives the soup a rich, creamy texture and the chilli, lemongrass and kaffir lime add a zesty kick. This vegetarian soup is suitable for vegans if you leave out the fish sauce.

Heat the olive oil in a large stockpot over medium heat. Add the onion, garlic, chilli, ginger, galangal, lemongrass, lime leaf and coriander root and sauté until fragrant. Add the coconut cream and bring to the boil.

Add the pumpkin and stock and return to the boil, then reduce the heat and simmer, covered, for 1 hour, or until the pumpkin is soft.

Leave to cool a little, then purée with a hand-held stick blender or transfer to a food processor and purée until smooth. Pass the soup through a fine chinois or fine mesh strainer into a large saucepan. Return to the boil and season with salt and fish sauce, to taste, if using.

Ladle the soup into serving bowls. Garnish with bean sprouts, coriander and Vietnamese mint leaves, and serve with a wedge of lime.

COOK'S TIPS

If you have time, roast the pumpkin beforehand for extra depth of flavour.

Spring

SPRING VEGETABLE MINESTRONE

Serves 4–6

200 g (7 oz) cannellini beans,
   soaked overnight
125 ml (4 fl oz/½ cup) olive oil
3 onions, finely chopped
3 garlic cloves, minced
   (see Cook's tips)
2 carrots, diced
2 celery stalks, diced
420 g (15 oz) tin diced tomatoes
1 bay leaf
1.5 litres (52 fl oz/6 cups) Vegetable
   stock (page 151)
100 g (3½ oz) kale, shredded
3 zucchini (courgettes), diced
125 g (4½ oz) green beans,
   chopped
chopped parsley, to serve
finely grated parmesan cheese,
   to serve

This lovely, light minestrone makes for a great vegetarian lunch (and for a vegan meal, simply leave out the parmesan cheese). You need to get this underway in advance, as the dried beans have to be soaked overnight.

~~~~~~~~~~~~

Drain the soaked cannellini beans, put them in a saucepan and cover with plenty of cold water. Bring to the boil, then reduce the heat to low and simmer for 1½ hours, or until the beans are soft and cooked through.

Heat the olive oil in a stockpot over medium heat. Add the onions and garlic and cook, stirring occasionally, for about 5 minutes, or until the onions are soft and translucent. Add the carrots and celery and cook for 3–5 minutes, or until soft.

Add the cooked beans, tomatoes, bay leaf and stock. Bring to the boil, then reduce the heat, cover and simmer for 1 hour. Add the kale, zucchini and green beans and simmer for a further 30 minutes.

Season to taste with sea salt and freshly ground pepper. Sprinkle with parsley and grated parmesan before serving.

COOK'S TIPS

Many of the recipes in this book call for minced garlic. You can either use a garlic crusher or do this by hand with a knife. If using a knife, thinly slice the garlic clove one way and then slice it the other. Continue chopping until the garlic is finely minced.

42

HERBS

~~~

We use an abundant variety of herbs in the kitchen at SoJo. They have such wonderful flavours and can be added to almost any dish. Although we have garden beds at the front of the café, we use so many herbs that we struggle to keep up with our own demand, so we also plant them in containers around the café. I love the look of big tins or boxes overflowing with sage, rosemary, oregano, thyme, or whatever is in season. The key to keeping them healthy and looking their best is to constantly rotate the containers so all the plants get a good amount of light. And they really need to be watered every day.

One of the most cost-effective ways to create visual impact when setting the scene for your own dining extravaganza is to use large display bunches of herbs, such as sage or rosemary. The herbs look great arranged in empty jam jars on the table, and they smell fantastic too. You can collect jars at home or buy them for a few cents from a thrift shop.

Putting a few pots of herbs on your windowsill or table is a great way to bring green into any indoor space. The plants can be cultivated fairly easily in your garden or bought from your local nursery or farmer's market.

CHICKEN SCHNITZEL WRAPS

Serves 4

Chicken schnitzels

150 g (5½ oz/1 cup) plain
 (all-purpose) flour
3 free-range eggs
100 ml (3½ fl oz) milk
120 g (4¼ oz/2 cups) panko
 breadcrumbs
1 tablespoon dried basil
12 chicken tenderloins
olive oil, for frying

For the wraps

4 x 25 cm (10 inch) tortillas
4 tablespoons Aïoli (page 111)
4 tablespoons Tomato relish
 (page 49)
2 tomatoes, sliced
8 slices of tasty cheese
2 handfuls of mixed lettuce leaves
 or ½ iceberg lettuce, shredded

Delicious and so easy to make, these wraps are an absolute crowd pleaser for all ages. They make great picnic food, too – just remember to drain the tomato well or the wraps will become soggy. The schnitzels are also delicious simply served with salad, vegetables or, my favourite, with braised red cabbage, potato salad and a few lemon wedges.

~~~~~~~~~

TO MAKE THE CHICKEN SCHNITZELS, put the flour in a bowl and season with sea salt and freshly ground pepper. In another bowl, whisk together the eggs and milk. In a third bowl, mix together the panko breadcrumbs and basil.

Dust each chicken tenderloin in the seasoned flour. Dip in the egg mix and then coat in breadcrumbs.

Place a large heavy-based frying pan over high heat. Pour the olive oil into the pan to a depth of 5 mm (¼ inch). When the oil is hot, add the crumbed chicken in batches and shallow-fry for 3 minutes on each side, or until the chicken is cooked through and the breadcrumbs are golden.

TO ASSEMBLE THE WRAPS, spread each tortilla with aïoli on one half and tomato relish on the other.

Top each tortilla with four slices of tomato, two slices of cheese, a small handful of lettuce and three chicken schnitzels. Roll up and cut in half diagonally to serve.

TOMATO RELISH

Makes about 1 litre (35 fl oz/4 cups)

1.5 kg (3 lb 5 oz) ripe tomatoes,
   chopped
2 large onions, chopped
340 g (12 oz/1½ cups) caster
   (superfine) sugar
375 ml (13 fl oz/1½ cups) malt
   vinegar
1 tablespoon curry powder
1 tablespoon mustard powder
1 teaspoon ground ginger
1 tablespoon salt
½ teaspoon chilli flakes

This condiment works well with just about everything: red meat, chicken, in a burger or with chips. It is simply a fabulous 'go-to' recipe that keeps well and adds a bit of zing to a meal.

Put the tomatoes and onions in a large saucepan with the sugar and vinegar. Bring to the boil, then reduce the heat and simmer, stirring often, for about 20 minutes, or until reduced and slightly thickened.

Mix the curry and mustard powders, ginger, salt and chilli flakes with 3 tablespoons water to make a paste. Stir into the tomato mixture and simmer for a further 5 minutes, or until thickened.

Store the tomato relish in clean jars in the fridge for up to 1 week or in sterilised jars for 1 month.

KASUNDI

Makes about 1 litre (35 fl oz/4 cups)

2 kg (4 lb 8 oz) ripe tomatoes, chopped
4 large onions, chopped
8 garlic cloves, roughly chopped
500 ml (17 fl oz/2 cups) apple
   cider vinegar
300 g (10½ oz/1⅓ cups, firmly
   packed) dark brown sugar
60 g (2¼ oz) sea salt
2 teaspoons ground ginger
2 teaspoons ground allspice
1 tablespoon ground turmeric
1 tablespoon mustard seeds
1 tablespoon cumin seeds
1 tablespoon coriander seeds
1 tablespoon nigella seeds
1 teaspoon chilli flakes

Kasundi is a wonderfully spiced relish with an exotic Indian flavour, which we use a lot. It works particularly well with fish, lamb and vegetarian dishes, and even as a side dish for roast vegetables.

Combine the tomatoes, onions and garlic in a large saucepan over medium heat. Add the vinegar, brown sugar and salt and bring to the boil.

Meanwhile, put all the spices in a frying pan over medium heat and cook, stirring, for 2 minutes, or until aromatic. Tip the spices into the tomato mixture, then reduce the heat to low and simmer, stirring frequently, until the mixture has reduced by about half. Allow to cool slightly, then blend with a hand-held stick blender or food processor.

Store the kasundi in clean jars in the fridge for up to 1 week or in sterilised jars for about 1 month.

ROAST CHICKEN AND LENTILS WITH ORANGE FENNEL SALAD

Serves 4

This chicken salad is great when you're busy, as the roast chicken and lentils can be cooked the day before. I sometimes make a vegetarian version, swapping the chicken for roast eggplant (aubergine), stuffed with the same pistachio and lemon mixture. The roast chicken and lentils makes a great meal for winter too, served with roast vegetables.

Lentils

250 g (9 oz) puy or tiny blue-green lentils
1 tablespoon red wine vinegar
1 tablespoon extra virgin olive oil,
　plus extra to serve

Roast chicken with pistachio and lemon stuffing

olive oil, for frying
1 small onion, diced
2 garlic gloves, minced
a pinch of chilli flakes
1/2 loaf of stale bread, torn into
　small pieces
50 g (1¾ oz) butter, softened
120 g (4¼ oz) pistachio nuts,
　roughly chopped
finely grated zest of 1 lemon
1 tablespoon chopped thyme
1 tablespoon chopped flat-leaf
　(Italian) parsley
1.5 kg (3 lb 5 oz) free-range chicken

Orange fennel salad

1 orange, or blood orange, peeled
　and segmented
16 asparagus spears, trimmed and
　blanched
1 small fennel bulb, thinly sliced
2 spring onions (scallions), thinly sliced
1 red witlof (chicory), washed and
　leaves picked
1 small handful of wild rocket (arugula)
House dressing (page 111), to taste

TO MAKE THE LENTILS, soak them in water for 2 hours, then drain. Put the lentils and 160 ml (5¼ fl oz) water in a saucepan and bring to the boil. Simmer, stirring occasionally, until all the water has been absorbed. Stir in the vinegar and olive oil and season with sea salt and freshly ground pepper.

TO MAKE THE ROAST CHICKEN WITH PISTACHIO AND LEMON STUFFING, heat a little olive oil in a frying pan over medium heat and sauté the onion for 5 minutes, or until translucent. Add the garlic and chilli and stir for a few more minutes, then transfer to a bowl and leave to cool a little. Add the bread, butter, pistachios, lemon zest, chopped herbs and season with salt and pepper. Stir to combine.

Preheat the oven to 220°C (425°F). Rinse and dry the chicken and then fill with the stuffing. Truss with kitchen string, season with salt and pepper and drizzle with a little olive oil. Place in a roasting tin, breast side up, and roast for 30 minutes. Reduce the oven to 180°C (350°F) and cook for a further 1 hour, or until the juices run clear. Leave for 10 minutes before carving.

TO MAKE THE ORANGE FENNEL SALAD, combine all the ingredients in a large bowl, adding the dressing to taste. Season with salt and pepper.

To serve, carve the chicken and arrange on four plates or a large platter. Take spoonfuls of the stuffing and break it over the chicken. Spoon some lentils onto each plate and drizzle with extra virgin olive oil. Serve with the orange and fennel salad.

SEARED SALMON WITH ASPARAGUS AND POACHED EGG

Serves 4

1 tablespoon olive oil
4 x 125 g (4½ oz) pieces salmon,
   pin-boned
4 free-range eggs
16 asparagus spears
16 cherry tomatoes, halved
½ small red onion, thinly sliced
1 bunch of watercress, sprigs picked
100 ml (3½ fl oz) Aïoli (page 111)
lemon wedges, to serve

The salmon here is cooked on the stove and then finished in the oven, but when we're on holiday we like to cook the fish outdoors on the barbecue. To make things easier, we prepare the salad and poach the eggs beforehand, indoors. To reheat the eggs, have a small pot of simmering water sitting beside your barbecue. When you are ready to serve, drop the poached eggs in the hot water for about 30 seconds to warm them up.

Preheat the oven to 180°C (350°F). Heat a large ovenproof, non-stick frying pan over high heat. Add the olive oil and fry the salmon, skin side down, for about 3 minutes, or until the skin is crispy and brown.

Carefully flip the salmon over and then place the pan in the oven and cook for a further 5 minutes. After this time, the salmon should be rare but not raw in the middle. Leave in the oven for an extra 2 minutes if you like your fish cooked through.

Meanwhile, poach the eggs for 2–4 minutes in a pan of simmering water (page 33).

To blanch the asparagus, bring a saucepan of water to the boil. Snap off and discard the woody ends from the asparagus, add to the boiling water and blanch for 1 minute. Refresh in a bowl of iced water, then drain.

Combine the asparagus, tomatoes, onion, watercress and aïoli in a large bowl. Divide the salad among four plates, then top with the salmon and a poached egg. Serve with a wedge of lemon.

LEMON CHICKEN, QUINOA TABOULEH AND MINTED YOGHURT

Serves 4

This is a great dish for those long, lazy spring lunches. Serve with a large jug of hot mint tea, made with fresh mint and hot water – or serve the tea chilled over ice on a hot day. I love the flavour of the spiced chicken skin, but you could use skinless fillets if you're concerned about cholesterol.

Lemon chicken

1 Preserved lemon (page 56)
100 ml (3½ fl oz) olive oil
1 tablespoon smoked paprika
1 teaspoon minced garlic
1 tablespoon chopped thyme
a pinch of chilli flakes
4 boneless chicken breast fillets,
    skin on

Quinoa tabouleh

200 g (7 oz) quinoa
16 cherry tomatoes, halved
2 small Lebanese (short)
    cucumbers, cubed
½ pomegranate, seeded
1 bunch of flat-leaf (Italian) parsley,
    leaves picked
1 small handful of mint leaves, torn
    if large
House dressing, to taste (page 111)

Minted yoghurt

200 g (7 oz) plain yoghurt
200 ml (7 fl oz) olive oil
2 tablespoons chopped mint
1 teaspoon minced garlic

TO MAKE THE LEMON CHICKEN, remove the preserved lemon from the brine and rinse it under cold water. Pat dry and then use a knife to remove the rind, discarding the flesh and white pith. Finely dice the lemon rind.

Combine the diced lemon rind, olive oil, paprika, garlic, thyme and chilli flakes in a large bowl. Season with sea salt and freshly ground pepper. Add the chicken and toss to coat in the marinade, then cover and refrigerate for 2 hours, or overnight.

Preheat the oven to 180°C (350°F). Heat an ovenproof, non-stick frying pan over high heat and cook the chicken, skin side down, for 5 minutes, then turn and cook for a further 3 minutes. Transfer the pan to the oven and cook for 10 minutes. Leave to rest in a warm place for 10 minutes.

TO MAKE THE QUINOA TABOULEH, put the quinoa and 200 ml (7 fl oz) water in a saucepan. Bring to the boil, then reduce the heat and simmer, covered, until all the water has been absorbed. Tip out onto a tray and allow to cool. Once cool, mix through the remaining tabouleh ingredients, adding the dressing to taste. Season with salt and pepper.

TO MAKE THE MINTED YOGHURT, blend all the ingredients together using a food processor or hand-held stick blender. Season to taste with salt and pepper.

To serve, spread a large dollop of minted yoghurt over each plate. Top with some quinoa tabouleh and a chicken breast.

PRESERVED LEMONS

Fills 2 x 1 litre (35 fl oz/4 cup) jars

500 g (1 lb 2 oz) sea salt
20 lemons (thick-skinned lemons
   are best)
2 bay leaves, torn into small pieces
4 cloves, crushed
6 bird's eye chillies, cut in half
   lengthways
2 tablespoons coriander seeds
about 200 ml (7 fl oz) extra
   lemon juice

I like to have a jar of preserved lemons in my kitchens at all times. They are such a fantastic long-life 'go-to' product, along with other ingredients such as salami, tinned tuna (ethically sourced of course), capers, tinned tomatoes and anchovies... the list goes on. With a well-stocked pantry you can whip up a tasty meal in minutes. I like to make this recipe in spring, when lemons are in season, so they can be bought relatively inexpensively and in bulk. As long as you stick to the recipe, these preserved lemons will keep for years in the pantry.

Sterilise two good-quality 1 litre (35 fl oz/4 cup) jars. Add 2 teaspoons of the salt to each jar and then set aside.

Scrub the lemons with a soft scrubbing brush. Cut the lemons into quarters and put them into a large plastic container. Add the remaining salt and mix together while really massaging the salt into the fruit. Add the bay leaves, cloves, chillies and coriander seeds, and work them through the mix.

With clean hands, place the lemons into the jars, arranging them so the skin side of the lemon is mostly visible to the outside, and pressing down on the fruit to expel as much liquid into the jar as possible. Add the extra lemon juice to the remaining salt mix in the container and then pour the juice and aromatics over the lemons in both jars until all the fruit is covered in liquid.

Clean the rims of the jars with a clean cloth dipped in boiling water. Seal the lids or caps tightly. The jars are best stored in a cool pantry or cupboard and not refrigerated. Leave the lemons for at least 1 month before using them. Refrigerate after use.

ARTICHOKE RISOTTO

Serves 4

2 globe artichokes
200 ml (7 fl oz) white wine
200 ml (7 fl oz) white wine vinegar
3 tablespoons caster (superfine) sugar

Risotto
1.5 litres (52 fl oz/6 cups) Vegetable
  stock (page 151)
2 tablespoons olive oil
1 small onion, finely diced
1 small leek, pale part only, finely diced
2 celery stalks, finely diced
1 teaspoon minced garlic
330 g (11½ oz/1½ cups) arborio rice
80 g (2¾ oz) butter
1 tablespoon chopped thyme
1 tablespoon chopped parsley
1 teaspoon finely grated lemon zest
100 g (3½ oz/1 cup) finely grated
  parmesan cheese
extra virgin olive oil, to serve

COOK'S TIPS

A non-reactive saucepan is one made from ceramic or stainless steel, which won't react when it comes into contact with acidic foods such as lemon juice, tomatoes or wine. A reaction between the metal and the food can alter the food's flavour, giving it a slight metallic taste.

We've used artichokes here, but this basic risotto is the starting point for an infinite array of combinations, limited only by your imagination and, of course, the best produce of the season.

TO PREPARE THE ARTICHOKES, trim them of all the tough outer leaves. Cut into quarters and remove the fibrous inner centres.

Combine 400 ml (14 fl oz) water with the wine, vinegar and sugar in a non-reactive saucepan (see Cook's tips). Add the artichokes and bring to the boil, then reduce the heat and simmer for about 20 minutes, or until tender. Drain and set aside to cool.

TO MAKE THE RISOTTO, bring the stock to the boil in a saucepan, then reduce the heat to low and keep at a simmer.

Heat the olive oil in a large heavy-based saucepan over medium heat. Add the onion, leek, celery and garlic and sauté for about 5 minutes, or until translucent. Add the rice and stir for a minute or two until well coated with the onion mixture.

Add the hot stock, a cupful at a time, stirring constantly until each cup of stock has been absorbed before adding another. Once you've added 4 cups, add the artichokes and another cup of stock. When the stock has been absorbed, check if the rice is al dente. You may want to add a little more stock, depending on your taste.

Stir in the butter, herbs, lemon zest and half the parmesan, and season with sea salt and freshly ground pepper. Divide the risotto among four bowls and drizzle with a little extra virgin olive oil. Serve the remaining parmesan on the side.

ORECCHIETTE WITH BROCCOLINI, OLIVES AND PANGRATTATO

Serves 4

500 g (1 lb 2 oz) orecchiette pasta
450 g (1 lb/2 bunches) broccolini
80 ml (2½ fl oz/⅓ cup) olive oil
30 g (1 oz/½ cup) fresh
   breadcrumbs
2 garlic gloves, minced
6 anchovy fillets
16 kalamata or other black olives,
   pitted
½ teaspoon chilli flakes
finely grated parmesan cheese,
   to serve

Orecchiette is the traditional pasta from the southern region of Italy. Its name translates as 'little ears', which refers to its distinctive shape. If you can't find orecchiette, use penne or spaghetti.

~~~~~~~~~~~~~~~~~~~~~~~~~~~~

Cook the pasta in a large saucepan of boiling salted water, following the manufacturer's instructions. Trim the broccolini and blanch in a saucepan of boiling water for 2 minutes, Drain, reserving 250 ml (9 fl oz/1 cup) of the cooking water. Refresh the broccolini in iced water.

Heat the olive oil in a frying pan over medium heat. Add the breadcrumbs and toss in the oil until golden and toasted. Remove from the pan and set aside.

In the same pan, sauté the garlic and anchovies for 3–5 minutes, until the garlic softens and the anchovies start to break down. Add the olives and chilli and heat through. Add the broccolini and toss to coat in the mixture.

Return the pasta to the large saucepan. Tip in the broccolini mixture and reheat over medium heat, adding a little of the reserved cooking water if the mixture seems too dry.

Divide among four bowls, season with sea salt and freshly ground pepper and sprinkle with the toasted breadcrumbs. Serve with grated parmesan.

MOROCCAN LAMB SALAD WITH RISONI

Serves 4

1 teaspoon ground cumin

1 teaspoon ground coriander

1 teaspoon ground fennel

1 teaspoon ground cinnamon

1 teaspoon chilli flakes

100 ml (3½ fl oz) olive oil, plus extra
for cooking

800 g (1 lb 12 oz) lamb backstraps
or loin fillets

500 g (1 lb 2 oz) risoni pasta

150 g (5½ oz/1 cup) peas, fresh
or frozen

2 handfuls of wild rocket (arugula)

200 g (7 oz) Salsa verde (page 88)

200 g (7 oz) Marinated feta,
crumbled (page 28)

Always a favourite and very easy to prepare, this lamb salad is a good basic recipe that can be made in large quantities for groups. For a delicious vegetarian version, substitute either roast pumpkin (winter squash) or tofu for the lamb.

Combine the spices and olive oil in a bowl. Season with sea salt and freshly ground pepper. Rub the marinade over the lamb, then cover and refrigerate for at least 2 hours, or preferably overnight.

Heat a chargrill pan or barbecue chargrill plate over high heat. Brush the pan with a little olive oil, then add the lamb and seal it on one side, cooking for 3 minutes. Turn the lamb over and cook for a further 2 minutes. Remove from the heat and leave to rest in a warm place for 5 minutes before slicing.

Meanwhile, cook the risoni in a saucepan of boiling salted water following the manufacturer's instructions. Blanch the peas in boiling water for 1–2 minutes. Refresh in iced water, then drain.

Combine the risoni, peas and rocket in a bowl and toss with the salsa verde. Add the sliced lamb and toss to combine. Divide among four plates, top with crumbled feta and season with salt and pepper.

CASARECCE WITH SPRING LAMB

Serves 4

Slow-cooked lamb shoulder

1 small onion, finely diced

1 carrot, finely diced

2 celery stalks, finely diced

2 garlic cloves, finely diced

1 tablespoon chopped thyme

2 large rosemary sprigs

4 bay leaves

1 tablespoon sea salt

1 tablespoon peppercorns, crushed
   in a mortar and pestle

1 tablespoon fennel seeds, crushed
   in a mortar and pestle

a pinch of chilli flakes

100 g (3½ oz) green olives,
   preferably Sicilian

1 orange, zest peeled into strips and
   then juiced

500 g (1 lb 2 oz) boned lamb
   forequarter (shoulder)

500 ml (17 fl oz/2 cups) white wine

Chicken stock, as needed (page 151)

500 g (1 lb 2 oz) casarecce pasta

chopped flat-leaf (Italian) parsley,
   to serve

shaved pecorino cheese, to serve

This is one of our favourite pastas. It's not too heavy and not too light: just right for spring. I like to scatter a handful of rocket (arugula), dressed with a little olive and balsamic vinegar, over each dish. The lamb needs to be roasted and then left overnight in the fridge, so make sure to plan ahead.

~~~~~~~~~~~~~~~~~~~~~~~~~~~~~~

TO MAKE THE SLOW-COOKED LAMB SHOULDER, preheat the oven to 170°C (325°F). Put all the vegetables, herbs, spices, olives, strips of orange zest and orange juice in a roasting tin. Place the lamb shoulder on top. Add the wine and top up with enough stock to nearly cover.

Cover with baking paper and foil, then place in the oven and roast for 3 hours. Remove the lamb from the oven, cover with a clean tea towel and set aside until cooled to room temperature. Transfer the lamb and tin to the fridge to cool overnight (or use immediately if you like). The following day, remove any fat that has congealed on the surface, then use your fingers to gently tear the lamb into bite-sized pieces.

Cook the pasta in a large pan of boiling salted water, following the manufacturer's instructions.

Meanwhile, reheat the lamb braise in a large saucepan and check the seasoning. Add the cooked pasta and toss until well combined and the pasta is coated in the sauce. Serve sprinkled with parsley, with the pecorino on the side.

VINTAGE BUTTER KNIVES

~~~

I love bone-handled knives. Although they don't tend to fare that well in dishwashers, especially commercial ones, they are worth the hand-washing because they look and feel so beautiful and unique. Spreading butter, jams, condiments and the like with beautiful vintage knives makes any mealtime seem more elegant.

I buy good-quality knives whenever I come across them at markets or antique shops (they usually only cost about as much as a cup of coffee). They look great stored en masse in a stoneware jar, with the blades facing down and the handles on display.

RICCIARELLI BISCUITS

Makes about 24

375 g (13 oz/3⅔ cups) almond meal
400 g (14 oz) caster (superfine)
   sugar
finely grated zest of 2 lemons
finely grated zest of ½ orange
90 ml (3 fl oz) egg whites (about 3)
1 teaspoon honey
icing (confectioners') sugar,
   for dusting

These delicious Italian almond biscuits should have a light, chewy texture and zesty lemon zing. You can easily double the quantities and freeze half the mixture, ready to make a batch on another day.

Preheat the oven to 180°C (350°F). Combine all the ingredients (except the icing sugar) in a large bowl to form a firm dough.

Divide the dough into four portions. Roll each one into a log about the diameter of an apricot. Cut the logs diagonally, about 5 mm (¼ inch) thick, to give you oval-shaped biscuits.

Line two baking trays with baking paper and dust with icing sugar. Arrange the biscuits on the trays and dust with more icing sugar.

Bake for 10–15 minutes, or until golden. Allow to cool a little on the trays before transferring to a wire rack to cool completely.

LEMON TART

Serves 12

Sweet shortcrust pastry

250 g (9 oz/1²/₃ cups) plain
   (all-purpose) flour
60 g (2¹/₄ oz/¹/₄ cup) caster
   (superfine) sugar
150 g (5¹/₂ oz) chilled unsalted
   butter, cubed
1 free-range egg
2 free-range egg yolks
egg wash (1 egg whisked with
   2 tablespoons milk)

Lemon filling

6 free-range eggs
250 g (9 oz/heaped 1 cup) caster
   (superfine) sugar
finely grated zest and juice of
   3 large lemons
200 ml (7 fl oz) thin (pouring) cream
icing (confectioners') sugar,
   for dusting

What better way to end a dinner party than with this classic lemon tart? Top with fresh strawberries and whipped cream, and serve leftovers for afternoon tea with a pot of earl grey.

~~~~~~~~~~

TO MAKE THE SWEET SHORTCRUST PASTRY, put the flour, sugar and butter in a food processor. Process until the mixture resembles fine breadcrumbs. Add the egg and egg yolks and pulse until the dough comes together in a ball. Tip out onto a work surface, cover in plastic wrap and refrigerate for 30 minutes.

Knead the dough on a floured work surface for a minute or two until smooth and pliable.

Grease and flour a 28 cm (11 inch) loose-based fluted tart (flan) tin. Roll out the dough to about 5 mm (¹/₄ inch) thick, then roll the dough around the rolling pin, lift and carefully lay it into the tin, gently pressing to fit. Refrigerate for 30 minutes.

Preheat the oven to 180°C (350°F). To blind bake the tart case, line it with foil and fill with baking beads or dried beans. Bake for 20 minutes, or until the pastry is just starting to colour. Remove the foil and baking beads. Brush the tart case with the egg wash and bake for a further 5 minutes.

TO MAKE THE LEMON FILLING, whisk together the eggs and sugar until pale and creamy. Add the lemon zest and lemon juice and mix well. Whisk in the cream and then pour into the tart case.

Bake at 180°C (350°F) for 35–40 minutes, or until the filling is just set. Allow to cool for 30 minutes before removing from the tin. Dust with icing sugar before serving.

EASY SALTED CARAMEL SAUCE

Makes 500 ml (17 fl oz/2 cups)

125 g (4½ oz) salted butter,
   chopped
½ vanilla bean
200 g (7 oz) light brown sugar
125 ml (4 fl oz/1½ cups) thickened
   (whipping) cream
½ teaspoon sea salt

Proceed with caution when making this devilishly good caramel sauce – it's quite rich and sweet, so a little bit does go a long way! Use on porridge, pancakes or French toast, in milkshakes, or drizzle over stewed apples and vanilla ice cream.

Melt the butter in a saucepan. Slit the vanilla bean down its length with a small sharp knife and scrape out as many of the tiny black seeds as you can into the melted butter.

Add the brown sugar, cream and salt and bring to the boil, stirring vigorously with a whisk. When all of the ingredients are well combined and the sauce takes on a rich caramel hue, set aside and leave to cool to room temperature before serving.

If you have left-over sauce, pour it into a storage container, cover with the lid and refrigerate for up to 1 week. Leave the sauce to come to room temperature before using it, or microwave for a few seconds until runny.

FLOURLESS ORANGE CAKE

Serves 12

2 large oranges, washed
6 free-range eggs
250 g (9 oz) caster (superfine)
  sugar
250 g (9 oz/2½ cups) almond meal
1 teaspoon baking powder
icing (confectioners') sugar,
  for dusting

Easy to make and with no oil, butter or flour, this cake scores very well on the healthy treat scale. Almond meal is a great alternative to flour in gluten-free cakes and biscuits.

~~~~~~~~~~~~~~~~~~~~~~~~~~~

Bring a large saucepan of water to the boil, add the whole oranges, then cover the pan and simmer over low heat for 2 hours.

Preheat the oven to 180°C (350°F). Butter and flour a 24 cm (9½ inch) spring-form cake tin.

Remove the oranges from the water and set aside to cool. When cool enough to handle, roughly chop, removing any seeds. Place the orange flesh in the food processor, add the eggs and process until smooth.

Combine the sugar, almond meal and baking powder in a large mixing bowl. Whisk in the orange mixture and pour into the tin.

Bake for 50 minutes, or until a skewer inserted into the middle of the cake comes out clean. Allow to cool in the tin before removing. Dust with icing sugar and serve with whipped cream.

02

SUMMER

SUMMER CONJURES UP IMAGES OF SUN-BLEACHED DAYS AND LONG HOT EVENINGS OUTDOORS

Sprinkler systems and lawn mowers; paddling pools and ice creams; picnics, cicadas and outdoor entertaining... everything seems to move at a more leisurely pace in summer.

When it comes to meals, we naturally tend to move towards lighter, thirst-quenching foods that have a higher water content, such as lettuce, tomatoes and melons. Summertime is also when we entertain outdoors – brunches, barbecue lunches, and even alfresco dinners under the stars, if we are lucky.

So open up the doors and windows, let in the warm summer breeze and get cooking.

SUMMER CARIBBEAN MULE

Serves 6

This is our SoJo version of the classic Moscow mule: a fantastic drink for the summer months. The combination of ingredients is punchy and refreshing and this has quickly become a favourite when friends come over to hang out.

24 ice cubes
6 limes, quartered
12 mint sprigs
180 ml (6 fl oz) good-quality vodka
1.2 litres (42 fl oz) ginger beer
1.2 litres (42 fl oz) fresh pineapple juice

Divide the ice among six 500 ml (17 fl oz/2 cup) glasses. Into each glass, squeeze the juice of 1 lime (4 quarters) and then throw in the left-over lime quarters. Rub two mint sprigs with your palms and add them to the glass.

Pour in 30 ml (1 fl oz) of vodka, then add 200 ml (7 fl oz) each of ginger beer and pineapple juice. Repeat with the remaining ingredients.

PEACH AND APRICOT CRUSH

Serves 4

With stone fruit in season, take the opportunity to create this refreshingly minty, citrusy beverage. Served over ice, it's a perfect drink to herald the warmer months.

2 tablespoons caster (superfine) sugar
4 peaches, stones removed, peeled and roughly chopped
8 apricots, stones removed, peeled and roughly chopped
24 ice cubes
2 tablespoons chopped mint
1 litre (35 fl oz/4 cups) freshly squeezed orange juice
extra ice cubes, to serve
small mint sprigs, to garnish

Put 200 ml (7 fl oz) water in a 2 litre (70 fl oz/8 cup) saucepan, along with the sugar, peaches and apricots. Stir well and place over high heat. Bring to the boil, then reduce the heat to low and simmer with the lid on for 5 minutes. Set aside to cool for an hour. Put four 350 ml (12 fl oz) glasses in the fridge to chill.

Pour half the mixture into a blender (one that is strong enough to crush ice). Add 12 ice cubes, 1 tablespoon chopped mint and 500 ml (17 fl oz/ 2 cups) of the orange juice. Blend for 30 seconds, or until all the ingredients are well combined.

Pour into two chilled glasses. Repeat with the remaining ingredients to make another two drinks. Add extra ice cubes and garnish with mint sprigs.

SUMMER EGGS

Serves 4

2 firm, ripe avocados
juice of ½ lemon
8 free-range eggs
8 slices of wholegrain bread
butter, for the toast
4 roma (plum) tomatoes, sliced
2 handfuls of baby English spinach
   leaves
100 g (3½ oz) Marinated feta
   (page 28)
4 tablespoons Pesto (page 88)

Oh-so-fresh and, as long as you've got the feta and pesto on hand, this has got to be one of the quickest and simplest breakfasts ever.

Cut the avocados in half, remove the stones and use a spoon to scoop the flesh into a small mixing bowl. Add the lemon juice and season with sea salt and freshly ground pepper. Use a fork to crush everything together and set aside.

Poach the eggs for 2–4 minutes in a pan of simmering water (page 33).

Meanwhile, toast the bread, spread with a little butter, then top with the crushed avocado.

Arrange the toast on four plates. Top with some sliced tomato, baby spinach and a poached egg. Crumble some feta over the top and drizzle with a little pesto. Season with salt and pepper.

GRANOLA WITH RHUBARB, APPLE AND YOGHURT

Serves 4

Granola
200 g (7 oz/2 cups) rolled
   (porridge) oats
55 g (2 oz/¾ cup) shredded coconut
80 g (2¾ oz/¾ cup) flaked almonds
40 g (1½ oz/¼ cup) pepitas
   (pumpkin seeds)
40 g (1½ oz/¼ cup) sunflower seeds
45 g (1½ oz/¼ cup) light brown sugar
60 ml (2 fl oz/¼ cup) honey

Baked rhubarb
3 kg (6 lb 12 oz) rhubarb, leaves
   removed, stems washed and cut
   into 2 cm (¾ inch) long batons
55 g (2 oz/¼ cup) caster
   (superfine) sugar
1 lemon, zest removed in strips with
   a peeler, then juiced
1 vanilla bean, split in half
   lengthways, seeds scraped

Vanilla yoghurt
1 vanilla bean
1 kg (2 lb 4 oz/4 cups) plain yoghurt
1 tablespoon caster (superfine) sugar

2 green apples, such as granny
   smiths, julienned
milk, to serve

Crunchy, textured and a delicious way to start the day, this granola can be made in bulk and stored in a cool, dry place in an airtight container. Some of my friends serve granola with fruit juice instead of milk and that seems to work well. Feel free to put your own stamp on the recipe by adding dried cranberries or apricots, or any other seeds you like.

TO MAKE THE GRANOLA, preheat the oven to 160°C (315°F). Combine all the ingredients and place on a baking tray. Bake for 8 minutes, then mix the ingredients again, making sure there aren't any bits stuck on the bottom of the tray.

Repeat the process four or five times, until the grains and seeds are toasted and golden brown. Allow to cool on the tray before storing in an airtight container.

TO MAKE THE BAKED RHUBARB, preheat the oven to 180°C (350°F). Place all the ingredients in an ovenproof dish and stir to combine and coat the rhubarb in the sugar. Cover with baking paper and foil and cook for 15–20 minutes, or until the rhubarb is soft but not mushy. Note that cooking times may vary, depending on the thickness of the rhubarb.

TO MAKE THE VANILLA YOGHURT, slit the vanilla bean down its length with a small sharp knife. Use the knife to scrape out as many of the tiny black seeds as you can into the yoghurt. Add the sugar and stir to combine.

To serve, place a cupful of granola in each bowl. Top with some rhubarb, vanilla yoghurt and julienned apple. Serve with milk on the side.

FRUIT SALAD WITH CHERRY YOGHURT

Serves 4

Cherry yoghurt

200 g (7 oz) cherries, pitted

500 g (1 lb 2 oz/2 cups) plain yoghurt

50 ml (1¾ fl oz) honey

Fruit salad

½ pineapple

½ honeydew melon

½ rockmelon (cantaloupe)

4 figs

4 apricots, stones removed

4 plums, stones removed

100 g (3½ oz) green grapes

125 g (4½ oz/½ punnet) strawberries

1 pear

small mint sprigs, to garnish

2 limes, halved

Summer is definitely the best season to enjoy a wide variety of fruit. Gorgeous produce is everywhere and nothing seems healthier or more delicious than a platter piled high. This fruit salad can be served all year round, of course; simply use whatever fruit is in season.

TO MAKE THE CHERRY YOGHURT, put the cherries in a small bowl with the yoghurt and honey. Combine well and set aside in the fridge for 1 hour.

TO MAKE THE FRUIT SALAD, cut the skin off the pineapple, slice and remove the core. Cut the pineapple into chunks about 2 cm (¾ inch) square. Put the pieces into a large mixing bowl.

Remove the skin and seeds from the honeydew and rockmelon and cut them into chunks the same size as the pineapple. Add the melon to the bowl. Cut each of the figs, apricots and plums into eight wedges. Cut the grapes and strawberries into quarters. Add to the bowl, then gently combine all the fruit.

Cut the pear lengthways into quarters and carefully remove the core with a paring knife. Cut each quarter into four wedges and set aside.

To serve, place a quarter of the mixed fruit and four pear wedges on each plate (this also looks great served on one platter or in a big glass bowl). Dollop three generous spoonfuls of cherry yoghurt randomly on the fruit, and garnish each with a few mint sprigs and half a lime. Serve immediately.

BLUEBERRY PANCAKES WITH NECTARINES

Serves 4

Pancake batter

500 ml (17 fl oz/2 cups) milk

2 free-range eggs

300 g (10½ oz/2 cups) self-raising
flour

110 g (3¾ oz/½ cup) caster
(superfine) sugar

a pinch of salt

Grilled nectarines

20 g (¾ oz) unsalted butter

4 nectarines, cut into quarters

1 tablespoon caster (superfine) sugar

40 g (1½ oz) unsalted butter

125 g (4½ oz/1 punnet) blueberries

4 tablespoons mascarpone cheese
(see Cook's tips)

4 tablespoons pure maple syrup

icing (confectioners') sugar, for dusting

COOK'S TIPS

*For a healthier alternative,
replace the mascarpone with
yoghurt or fresh ricotta cheese.*

I often make these pancakes when we're on holiday, especially when my friend's daughters, Bella and Lina, come to stay. I can get these on the table in about 15 minutes, as the girls always seem to get up early and need to be fed instantly. Then, truth be known, I go back to bed!

TO MAKE THE PANCAKE BATTER, whisk the milk and eggs together. Combine the flour, sugar and salt in a large mixing bowl. Make a well in the centre of the flour and then slowly add the milk mixture, whisking continuously. Try to beat out all the lumps (you can use an electric mixer to do this if you prefer). Ideally, set the batter aside for an hour.

TO MAKE THE GRILLED NECTARINES, melt the butter in a chargrill pan or heavy-based frying pan over high heat. When the butter starts to sizzle, sprinkle the cut side of the nectarines with the sugar, then place them in the hot pan, cut side down. Cook for 2–3 minutes, until the nectarines start to caramelise. Remove from the heat and keep warm.

TO COOK THE PANCAKES, heat a large heavy-based frying pan over medium heat. Add a little butter and, when it starts to sizzle, spoon in enough batter to make a 4 cm (1½ inch) round. You should be able to fit three or four pancakes in the pan at a time, remembering to space each pancake apart, as the batter will spread a little as it cooks.

Dot the batter with blueberries. Once bubbles start to form in the batter, flip the pancakes over and cook the other side for 1 minute. Remove from the pan and keep warm while you cook the remaining batter. You should get about 12 pancakes from this quantity of batter.

To serve, place three pancakes on each plate and top with the grilled nectarines and a spoonful of mascarpone. Drizzle with maple syrup, dust with icing sugar and scatter with any remaining berries.

TEA

~~~

Although we are famed for loving our coffee in Melbourne, I also enjoy sitting down with a good cup of tea, as do many of my friends.

I have always loved the ceremonial aspect of tea drinking and at SoJo we serve our loose-leaf teas and herbal brews in silver teapots. The teapots have become a real talking point for our customers. I've collected many pots over the years, from charity shops, vintage markets, second-hand dealers, you name it.

Before I buy any teapot, there's a strict set of criteria that it has to meet: it needs to look good, be in a hygienic condition and, most importantly, it has to pour well. Over the years I've had a lot of strange looks from salespeople when I request a cup of water, to test the teapot for any holes and check the spout pours to my standards!

Beautiful teapots are great to have at home, too. Whether it's classic earl grey, English breakfast or sprigs of fresh mint added to boiling water, a cup of tea seems so much nicer when it's served from a beautiful vintage pot.

At home, I also keep a collection of milk jugs, sugar bowls, tea strainers and trays, to make sharing a cuppa with friends all the more special.

CORN AND ZUCCHINI FRITTERS

Serves 4

Corn and zucchini fritters

4 cobs of fresh corn
olive oil
2 zucchini (courgettes), grated
1 red onion, finely diced
½ bunch of coriander (cilantro),
    leaves picked and roughly chopped
2 free-range eggs
150 g (5½ oz/1 cup) self-raising
    flour

4 free-range eggs
2 firm, ripe avocados
juice of ½ lemon
200 ml (7 fl oz) Kasundi (page 49)
4 tablespoons sour cream
pea shoots or micro herbs,
    to garnish
smoked salmon or fried bacon,
    to serve (optional)

This recipe is our best-selling dish, hands down – it has icon status. In fact, I would go so far as to say that it generates about 20 per cent of our kitchen sales. We hope you like it as much as we do!

TO MAKE THE CORN AND ZUCCHINI FRITTERS, preheat the oven to 180°C (350°F). Place the corn cobs on a baking tray, drizzle with a little olive oil and roast for 45 minutes. Allow to cool, then use a sharp knife to remove the corn kernels from the cobs.

Place the corn, zucchini, onion and coriander in a large bowl. Add the eggs and flour and mix well. Season with sea salt and freshly ground pepper.

Heat 200 ml (7 fl oz) of olive oil in a large heavy-based frying pan over high heat. Using an ice cream scoop, scoop balls of the fritter mixture and add to the hot oil. Gently press the fritters down with the back of the scoop to flatten them slightly. Take care, as the oil can spit.

Cook the fritters for 2 minutes on one side, then turn them over and cook for a further 2 minutes, or until golden brown and cooked through. This amount of batter should make 12 fritters.

Poach the eggs for 2–4 minutes in a pan of simmering water (page 33).

Meanwhile, cut the avocados in half, remove the stones and then use a spoon to scoop the flesh into a small mixing bowl. Add the lemon juice and season with salt and pepper. Use a fork to crush everything together and set aside.

To serve, spread 2 heaped tablespoons of kasundi over each plate and top with three corn fritters. Top with some avocado, a poached egg and some sour cream and garnish with pea shoots. Serve with a side of smoked salmon or fried bacon if the troops are hungry.

PESTO

Makes about 350 g (12 oz)

125 ml (4 fl oz/½ cup) extra virgin
    olive oil
80 g (2¾ oz/½ cup) pine nuts
100 g (3½ oz/2 cups, firmly packed)
    basil leaves
3 garlic cloves, roughly chopped
½ teaspoon sea salt
60 g (2¼ oz) parmesan cheese,
    finely grated

If you have pesto and pasta on hand, you can have a quick and tasty meal ready in minutes. I like to keep pesto in the fridge to use as a dip, a spread for crusty bread, to add to a salad dressing or to dollop into home-made minestrone.

Heat 1 teaspoon of the olive oil in a small frying pan over medium heat. Add the pine nuts and cook for 3 minutes. Remove from the pan and set aside.

Put the basil, garlic, pine nuts and sea salt in a food processor and process until well combined. Add the parmesan and, with the motor running, add the remaining olive oil in a slow, steady stream until a coarse paste forms. Season to taste with sea salt and freshly ground pepper.

Store any left-over pesto in an airtight container in the fridge for up to 1 week. Before storing, the pesto needs to be covered with a good layer of olive oil, about 2 mm (¹⁄₁₆ inch) thick, to prevent it from browning.

SALSA VERDE

Makes about 600 g (1 lb 5 oz)

1 bunch of flat-leaf (Italian) parsley,
    leaves picked
½ bunch of mint, leaves picked
1 small garlic clove, peeled
juice of ½ lemon
2 small slices of sourdough, crusts
    removed, roughly chopped
1–2 anchovy fillets (optional)
350 ml (12 fl oz) olive oil

Another one of our kitchen staples, this 'go-to' green sauce really packs a punch. It's perfect with eggs at breakfast, grilled tuna at lunch or to dress green beans at dinner time. Leave out the anchovies for a vegan version of this classic sauce.

Put the herbs, garlic, lemon juice, bread and anchovies, if using, in a food processor and process until well combined. With the motor running, add the olive oil in a slow, steady stream until all the oil has been incorporated. Season with sea salt and freshly ground pepper.

Transfer the salsa verde to an airtight container, cover and store in the fridge for up to 5 days.

BASQUE EGGS

Serves 4

Stewed capsicum

20 g (¾ oz) butter

1 tablespoon olive oil

1 small onion, sliced

1 teaspoon minced garlic

2 red capsicums (peppers), sliced

1 teaspoon paprika

1 teaspoon ground cumin

1 teaspoon red wine vinegar
or sherry vinegar

1 teaspoon sugar

8 free-range eggs

80 ml (2½ fl oz/⅓ cup) thin
(pouring) cream

50 g (1¾ oz) butter

100 g (3½ oz) goat's cheese

8 slices of sourdough, toasted
and buttered

4 tablespoons Salsa verde
(page 88)

8 slices of smoked salmon or fried
bacon, to serve (optional)

This dish uses the delicious combination of flavours of slow-cooked sweet capsicum (pepper), creamy scrambled eggs, the bite of the goat's cheese and earthiness of the herbs in the salsa verde. Add a side of smoked salmon or crispy bacon, or top with some grilled asparagus for a vegetarian treat.

TO MAKE THE STEWED CAPSICUM, heat the butter and olive oil in a heavy-based saucepan over medium heat. Add the onion and garlic and sauté until the onion is a deep golden brown.

Add the capsicums, paprika, cumin, vinegar and sugar. Mix through and continue cooking for about 20 minutes, or until the capsicums are soft and most of the liquid has evaporated. Season with sea salt and freshly ground pepper. The stewed capsicums will keep in the fridge for about 4 days and are great as an accompaniment to cold meats or hard cheeses, so don't be afraid of making a little extra.

To prepare the scrambled eggs, whisk the eggs and cream in a bowl and season with salt and pepper. Heat half the butter in a large non-stick frying pan over medium heat. When the butter begins to sizzle, pour in half the egg mixture. Add 2 heaped tablespoons of stewed capsicum and half the goat's cheese. Using a wooden spatula, gently stir the capsicum and cheese through the eggs. Push the cooked egg towards the centre of the pan, tilting the pan to allow the uncooked egg to touch the base. Cook for 2 minutes, or until the eggs are just set. Remove from the pan and keep warm. Repeat with the remaining butter, egg mixture, capsicum and cheese.

Arrange the buttered toast on four plates, top with the scrambled eggs and drizzle with the salsa verde. If you like, serve with smoked salmon or bacon for a more substantial and decadent brunch.

FRIED EGGS WITH KAISERFLEISCH

Serves 4

12 Slow-roasted roma (plum)
    tomatoes (page 93)
50 ml (1¾ fl oz) pure maple syrup
1 tablespoon dijon mustard
500 g (1 lb 2 oz) piece kaiserfleisch,
    cut into 4 thick pieces
80 ml (2½ fl oz/⅓ cup) olive oil
20 g (¾ oz) butter
8 free-range eggs
8 slices of sourdough, toasted
    and buttered
micro herbs or shiso leaves,
    to garnish

A hearty breakfast indeed! The richness of the tomatoes, hint of rosemary, creaminess of the egg yolks and crunch of the toast make for a winning combination. Kaiserfleisch is a German thick-cut ham made from the eye of the pork loin – bacon makes a good substitute.

Preheat the oven to 130°C (250°F). Put the roasted tomatoes on a baking tray and place in the oven to warm up.

Combine the maple syrup and mustard in a small mixing bowl. Season with sea salt and freshly ground pepper.

Heat a chargrill pan or heavy-based frying pan over medium heat. Using a pastry brush, coat the kaiserfleisch with the maple and mustard mixture. Add the kaiserfleisch to the hot pan, then reduce the heat to low and cook for about 10 minutes, or until the outside is caramelised but not burnt. Remove from the pan and keep warm.

Heat half the olive oil and half the butter in a large non-stick frying pan over high heat. Add four eggs to the pan and fry until the whites are opaque and the edges are crisp (page 32). Repeat with the remaining oil, butter and eggs.

Arrange the buttered toast on four plates and top with a fried egg. Place a slice of kaiserfleisch and three tomato halves on each plate. Garnish with micro herbs or shiso.

SLOW-ROASTED ROMA TOMATOES

Makes 1 kg (2 lb 4 oz)

1 kg (2 lb 4 oz) roma (plum)
    tomatoes, halved lengthways
1 garlic bulb, broken into cloves
    and peeled
1 small handful of rosemary leaves
1 tablespoon balsamic vinegar
2 tablespoons extra virgin olive oil

My grandmother lived in Brunswick, in an area popular with many migrant families. As a child, I remember being fascinated by the large amount of produce these industrious people could grow in their tiny, mostly concreted, backyards. Grapes, artichokes and lemons were just the start. And the tomatoes – big, red, juicy organic tomatoes! Here's a simple recipe for a delicious summer staple.

Preheat the oven to 110°C (225°F). Line a large baking tray with baking paper.

Put the tomatoes, garlic and rosemary in a bowl. Season with sea salt and freshly ground pepper and drizzle with the vinegar and olive oil. Toss together, then arrange the tomatoes and garlic on the tray. Drizzle with the juices left in the bowl.

Roast in the oven for about 3 hours, or until the tomatoes are soft and caramelised around the edges. Store in the fridge for up to 4 days.

VINE TOMATOES WITH BUFFALO MOZZARELLA AND BASIL

Serves 4

8 slices of sourdough, toasted
extra virgin olive oil
8 vine-ripened tomatoes, sliced
1 buffalo mozzarella
1 small handful of basil leaves
good-quality aged balsamic
    vinegar

There is that moment in late summer when tomatoes are at their best, so make the most of them. Look out for heirloom varieties, such as Black Russian, Green Zebra and Pink Bumblebee.

Place two slices of toast on each plate and drizzle with a little olive oil. Arrange the sliced tomato on top of the toast.

Break the buffalo mozzarella into four pieces and place one on each plate. Tear the basil leaves and scatter them over the mozzarella, then drizzle with olive oil and balsamic vinegar. Finish with a pinch of sea salt and a good grind of black pepper.

CHICKEN NOODLE SOUP

Serves 4–6

4 large dried shiitake mushrooms
250 g (9 oz) egg noodles
1 tablespoon olive oil
1 garlic clove, minced
1 cm (½ inch) piece of fresh ginger,
    peeled and finely chopped
1 bird's eye chilli, thinly sliced
1 tablespoon light soy sauce
1 tablespoon rice wine
2 litres (70 fl oz/8 cups) Chicken
    stock (page 151)
200 g (7 oz) boneless, skinless
    chicken breast fillet, poached
    and shredded (page 166)
100 g (3½ oz) corn kernels (shaved
    off a cob of corn)
4 baby bok choy (pak choy),
    trimmed, leaves separated
2 spring onions (scallions),
    shredded, to garnish

This is light, full bodied and fresh – and our take on this classic Asian comfort food.

Soak the mushrooms in warm water for 30 minutes. Drain, discard the stems and thinly slice the caps. Meanwhile, cook the egg noodles following the manufacturer's instructions. Drain and set aside.

Heat the olive oil in a heavy-based saucepan large enough to hold all the ingredients. Add the mushrooms, garlic, ginger and chilli and sauté over medium heat for 3–4 minutes without colouring.

Stir in the soy sauce and rice wine, then add the stock and bring to the boil. Add the noodles, chicken, corn and bok choy and return to the boil. Season with sea salt and freshly ground pepper.

To serve, lift the noodles out first and divide among soup bowls, then top with the soup and remaining ingredients. Garnish with spring onion.

ZUCCHINI AND BACON SOUP

Serves 4–6

2 tablespoons olive oil

1 onion, finely diced

2 garlic cloves, minced

4 bacon rashers, cut into lardons

1 teaspoon ground cumin

2 zucchini (courgettes), diced
  or julienned

2 litres (70 fl oz/8 cups) Chicken
  stock (page 151)

110 g (3¾ oz/½ cup) risoni pasta

4 tablespoons Pesto, to serve
  (page 88) (optional)

I love to serve this – my favourite soup – as
a starter at dinner parties. If you like things zesty,
squeeze in a little lemon juice before serving, or add
decadence with a dollop of sour cream – or both.

Heat the olive oil in a large saucepan over high
heat. Add the onion and garlic and sauté until
translucent. Add the bacon and cumin and continue
to cook until the bacon has browned. Add the
zucchini and stir to combine.

Pour in the stock and bring to the boil, then add
the risoni. Simmer for about 10 minutes, or until the
risoni is cooked. Season with sea salt and freshly
ground pepper. Serve in soup bowls topped with
a tablespoon of pesto, if using.

CHICKEN AND PISTACHIO TERRINE

Makes 12 slices

20 g (¾ oz) butter

1 small onion, finely chopped

4 garlic cloves, finely chopped

150 g (5½ oz) chicken livers, cleaned, rinsed in milk and roughly chopped

100 ml (3½ fl oz) cognac

300 g (10½ oz) boneless, skinless chicken thigh fillets, roughly chopped

400 g (14 oz) boneless, skinless chicken breast fillets, diced

120 g (4¼ oz) minced (ground) pork

120 g (4¼ oz) minced (ground) chicken

100 g (3½ oz) baby English spinach leaves, chopped

1 tablespoon green peppercorns

55 g (2 oz/¾ cup, firmly packed) fresh breadcrumbs made from day-old bread

150 g (5½ oz/1 cup) shelled pistachio nuts

2 sage leaves, thinly sliced

finely grated zest of 2 lemons

1½ teaspoons Maldon sea salt

freshly ground pepper

1 egg, lightly beaten

250 g (9 oz) prosciutto, rindless but with lots of fat

Chicken terrine is perfect with a glass of rosé for a lazy, grazing lunch with friends – or jammed between a couple of pieces of crusty bread.

~~~~~~~~~~~~~~~~~~~~~~~~~~~~~~~~

Heat the butter in a heavy-based frying pan over high heat. Add the onion and garlic and sauté for 3 minutes, or until the onion is soft. Add the livers and cognac and sauté for a further minute. Transfer the liver mixture to a large mixing bowl. Add all the remaining ingredients, except the prosciutto, and mix together well.

Preheat the oven to 180°C (350°F). Line a 7 cm (2¾ inch) deep, 10 x 30 cm (4 x 12 inch) terrine dish with the prosciutto, overlapping each piece. Allow extra on the sides to fold over at the end.

Fill the terrine dish with the mixture and then fold over the prosciutto to completely enclose. Place a piece of baking paper over the top and put the terrine dish into a large baking dish half-filled with hot water.

Transfer to the oven and bake for 1 hour, or until the terrine is firm to touch. Remove from the oven and refrigerate overnight, with a weight sitting on top of it.

Remove the terrine from the fridge and cut into 2 cm (¾ inch) thick slices. Serve with cornichons and toast.

LINEN

~~~

Linen tablecloths and napkins will always add an air of sophistication to a table setting, especially if you use natural-toned cloths. Some people prefer to iron their linen table settings, but I like to let the rustic texture show through. So, after use I generally just machine-wash my linen on a gentle setting and dry it on a flat surface to minimise the creases. Then I fold it up as soon as it is dry.

Instead of buying tablecloths, I also sometimes just choose linen off a roll, by the metre, from a fabric store and then hem the edges (or not – depending on the material and what sort of look I'm trying to achieve).

Another trick that works well is to tailor and hem ripped or worn linen sheets or quilt covers to turn them into tablecloths and napkins. I am no good on a sewing machine, but I know people who are – luckily!

100

B.L.A.T

Serves 4

2 firm, ripe avocados
juice of ½ lemon
1 tablespoon olive oil
16 bacon rashers
4 Turkish pide breads
4 tablespoons Aïoli (page 111)
1 handful of mixed lettuce leaves
  or shredded iceberg
2 vine-ripened tomatoes, sliced

Kids love it, adults love it and we love the B.L.A.T too. I enjoy this toasted sandwich just as much when I use smoked salmon instead of bacon for a change. It's also delicious with the addition of a fried egg.

Cut the avocados in half, remove the stones and use a spoon to scoop the flesh into a small mixing bowl. Add the lemon juice and season with sea salt and freshly ground pepper. Use a fork to crush everything together.

Heat the olive oil in a heavy-based frying pan over medium heat and cook the bacon in batches. Drain on paper towel.

Slice the Turkish breads in half and lightly toast under a grill or in a toaster. Spread half the toast slices with crushed avocado and the other half with aïoli. Fill the sandwiches with bacon, lettuce and tomato and cut in half to serve.

SLOW-COOKED LAMB WITH PEARL COUSCOUS SALAD

Serves 4

Caramelised onions

2 small red onions

2 tablespoons light brown sugar

2 tablespoons red wine vinegar

2 tablespoons olive oil

---

2 tablespoons currants

500 g (1 lb 2 oz) Slow-cooked lamb
   shoulder (page 62)

500 g (1 lb 2 oz) pearl couscous

olive oil, for frying

2 eggplants (aubergines), cut into
   1 cm (½ inch) thick slices

1 handful of wild rocket (arugula)

1 small handful of mint leaves,
   roughly torn

1 small handful of flat-leaf (Italian)
   parsley leaves, roughly torn

½ pomegranate, seeded

200 ml (7 fl oz) Tahini yoghurt
   dressing (page 161)

4 tablespoons Pistachio dukkah
   (page 189)

As meat prices increase, many of us are looking for ways to use secondary, cheaper, cuts of meat. Most of these are best cooked at a low temperature for hours, only needing to be checked occasionally, until the meat is rendered tender and succulent. Although we tend to think of a slow roast as a winter meal, it can be just as good in the warmer months, served as part of a salad, with simple vegetables and grains, or tossed through pasta.

~~~~~~~~~~

TO MAKE THE CARAMELISED ONIONS, preheat the oven to 180°C (350°F). Cut each onion into eight wedges and put in a bowl with the brown sugar, vinegar and olive oil. Toss to coat, then spread the onion wedges out on a small baking tray and roast for 20–25 minutes, until the onion is softened and caramelised around the edges.

Meanwhile, put the currants in a heatproof bowl, cover with hot water and set aside to soak for 10 minutes. Drain.

Roughly chop or shred the cooked lamb shoulder and set aside. Cook the couscous following the manufacturer's instructions.

Heat a non-stick frying pan over medium heat and add 1 tablespoon of the olive oil. Gently fry the eggplant slices, in batches, until golden brown. Remove and drain on paper towel.

Put the lamb, couscous and currants in a large bowl. Add the caramelised onion, fried eggplant, rocket, herbs and pomegranate seeds. Drizzle with the tahini yoghurt dressing and toss together. Season with sea salt and freshly ground pepper.

Divide the lamb and couscous salad among four bowls. Sprinkle 1 tablespoon of dukkah over the top of each salad before serving.

SEARED TUNA NICOISE

Serves 4

4 free-range eggs
4 kipfler (fingerling) potatoes,
    peeled
200 g (7 oz) green beans
olive oil, for cooking
4 x 150 g (5½ oz) tuna steaks
    (or use salmon)
50 g (1¾ oz/⅓ cup) pitted
    kalamata olives
½ small red onion, thinly sliced
1 tablespoon baby capers, rinsed
2 baby cos (romaine) lettuces,
    leaves picked
1 small handful of flat-leaf (Italian)
    parsley leaves, roughly chopped
House dressing, to taste (page 111)
8 anchovy fillets
lemon wedges, to serve

Here is our version of the classic salade niçoise. It's the perfect summer salad, especially served with a glass of crisp chardonnay. We always ensure that the tuna we use is ethically sourced, as are all the animal products we use.

Cook the eggs in a small saucepan of simmering water for 4 minutes, or until soft-boiled. Peel the eggs when they are cool enough to handle.

Cook the potatoes in a saucepan of boiling water for 5–10 minutes, or until tender. When cool, cut into thick slices. Meanwhile, blanch the beans in boiling water for 3–4 minutes. Refresh in a bowl of iced water, then drain.

Heat a chargrill pan or heavy-based frying pan over high heat, then add a little olive oil. Season the tuna with sea salt and freshly ground pepper and place in the hot pan. Cook for 3 minutes, then turn the tuna over and cook for a further 3 minutes. Depending on its thickness, this should give you tuna that is still pink in the middle; however, you may prefer to repeat the cooking process if you like your tuna cooked through. Keep the tuna warm while you make the salad.

Put the sliced potatoes, beans, olives, onion, capers, cos leaves and parsley in a large bowl. Add enough dressing to lightly coat the potato salad ingredients and toss to combine.

Divide the salad among four plates and top with a piece of tuna and a soft-boiled egg. Season with salt and pepper. Garnish with two anchovy fillets and serve with a lemon wedge.

TURKISH PIDE WITH ARTICHOKE AND LEEK

Serves 4

2 globe artichokes
200 ml (7 fl oz) white wine
200 ml (7 fl oz) white wine vinegar
3 tablespoons caster (superfine)
   sugar
40 g (1½ oz) butter
1 tablespoon olive oil
1 small onion, diced
1 teaspoon minced garlic
a pinch of chilli flakes
4 leeks, pale parts only, thinly sliced
4 Turkish pide breads
4 slices of taleggio cheese
1 handful of baby English spinach
   leaves

Melty, gooey and delicious, this is a perfect snack or late supper. It's simple to make, has only a few ingredients and is easily adapted to suit your appetite and your pantry. You could use rocket (arugula) instead of spinach, brie instead of taleggio, or slip in a slice of leg ham or prosciutto. If you don't have time to prepare artichokes from scratch, you can use good-quality deli-bought artichoke hearts.

To prepare the artichokes, trim them of all the tough outer leaves. Cut into quarters and remove the fibrous inner centres.

Combine 400 ml (14 fl oz) water with the wine, vinegar and sugar in a non-reactive saucepan. Add the artichokes. Bring to the boil, then reduce the heat and simmer for about 20 minutes, or until tender. Drain and set aside to cool.

Heat the butter and olive oil in a heavy-based saucepan over medium heat. Add the onion, garlic and chilli flakes and sauté for 3 minutes, or until the onion is soft. Add the leeks and continue to cook until the leeks are soft and most of the liquid has evaporated. Set aside to cool.

Cut the pide breads in half and lightly toast them under a grill (broiler) or in a toaster.

Spread each toasted pide base with the braised leeks, top with some sliced artichoke hearts and season with sea salt and freshly ground pepper. Add a slice of cheese, some spinach leaves and then place the pide lids on top. Cut in half to serve.

CHICKEN CAESAR SALAD

Serves 4

I have known even the most ardent anchovy haters be persuaded by a great Caesar! To make the salad even tastier, we like to cook the chicken and croutons with lemon thyme.

~~~~~~~~~~~~~~~~~~~~~~~~~~~~~~~~~

Dressing

2 garlic cloves, roughly chopped

2 teaspoons dijon mustard

pinch of sea salt

3 free-range egg yolks

2 teaspoons lemon juice

250 ml (9 fl oz/1 cup) olive oil

4 anchovy fillets, finely chopped

Caesar salad

2 garlic cloves, minced

2 tablespoons lemon thyme, chopped

1 teaspoon chilli flakes (optional)

80 ml (2½ fl oz/⅓ cup) olive oil, plus extra for frying

2 thick slices of sourdough, cut into 1 cm (½ inch) cubes

4 boneless, skinless chicken breast fillets

4 bacon rashers or pancetta (about 300 g/10½ oz), cut into lardons

4 free-range eggs

2 baby cos (romaine) lettuces, leaves picked

8 anchovy fillets

100 g (3½ oz) parmesan cheese, shaved with a potato peeler

extra lemon thyme, to garnish

TO MAKE THE DRESSING, put all the ingredients, except the olive oil and anchovies, in a food processor and blend for 30 seconds. With the motor running, add the olive oil in a slow, steady stream – the dressing will start to thicken and become creamy. Stir in the anchovies and taste for seasoning.

TO MAKE THE CAESAR SALAD, preheat the oven to 180°C (350°F). Combine the garlic, lemon thyme, chilli and olive oil in a large bowl. Season with sea salt and freshly ground pepper. Add the bread cubes and toss to coat in the mixture. Spread on a baking tray and toast in the oven for 10–15 minutes, until golden.

Place the chicken in the bowl and coat with the remaining lemon thyme mixture. Heat a little oil in a heavy-based, ovenproof frying pan over medium heat and cook the chicken for 6 minutes, then turn and cook for a further 4 minutes. Transfer the pan to the oven and cook for 5 minutes, or until the juices run clear from the thickest part of the breast. Transfer the chicken to a plate and leave to rest in a warm place for 10 minutes before slicing.

In the same frying pan, cook the bacon until crispy. Drain on paper towel.

Cook the eggs in a small saucepan of simmering water for 4 minutes, or until soft-boiled. Peel the eggs when they are cool enough to handle.

To assemble the salad, toss together the chicken, bacon and cos leaves with 250 ml (9 fl oz/1 cup) of the dressing. Serve topped with the anchovies and the eggs, cut in half so the yolks start to ooze. Garnish with parmesan and lemon thyme.

AIOLI

Makes about 650 ml (22½ fl oz)

4 garlic cloves
1 tablespoon dijon mustard
pinch of sea salt
6 free-range egg yolks
   (see Cook's tips)
1 tablespoon lemon juice
500 ml (17 fl oz/2 cups) olive oil

COOK'S TIPS

● *Use the left-over egg whites in an egg white omelette, filled with steamed broccolini, pesto and cottage cheese.*
● *If your aïoli does split, don't worry, there is a way to fix it. Place another egg yolk in a clean bowl. Using a whisk, slowly work your split mixture into the yolk, a few drops at a time, to bring it back to the correct consistency.*

This is our version of the classic garlic mayonnaise. In the café it gets used with potato wedges and chips, meat, vegetables, sandwiches, breakfast dishes... so many things. Try adding chopped herbs, such as tarragon, oregano or basil, for added zest.

Roughly chop the garlic and place in a food processor. Add the remaining ingredients, except the olive oil, and blend for 30 seconds, or until well combined.

With the motor running, add the olive oil in a slow, steady stream, just a few drops at a time so the mixture doesn't split (see Cook's tips). The aïoli will start to thicken and become creamy. When all of the oil has been added, remove the aïoli with a spatula and transfer to an airtight storage container or squeeze bottle ready for use. Store in the fridge for up to 5 days.

HOUSE DRESSING

Makes about 500 ml (17 fl oz/2 cups)

125 ml (4 fl oz/½ cup) white
   balsamic vinegar
1 tablespoon dijon mustard
1 garlic clove, roughly chopped
350 ml (12 fl oz) olive oil

This all-round dressing is great to have on hand for simple salads. Use it sparingly though, as the flavours are strong. Less is more here.

In a small food processor, blend together the vinegar, mustard and garlic. With the motor running, add the olive oil in a slow, steady stream until all the oil has been incorporated. Season with sea salt and freshly ground pepper. Store in a sterilised glass container in the fridge for up to 3 months.

LINGUINE WITH PRAWNS, CHILLI AND GARLIC

Serves 4

500 g (1 lb 2 oz) linguine
40 g (1½ oz) butter
2 tablespoons olive oil
1 small onion, diced
1 tablespoon minced garlic
20 raw tiger prawn (shrimp) tails,
    shelled and butterflied
4 roma (plum) tomatoes, diced
1 bird's eye chilli, thinly sliced,
    or 1 teaspoon chilli flakes
100 ml (3½ fl oz) dry white wine
2 tablespoons chopped basil
extra virgin olive oil, to serve

The tomato, onion, garlic, chilli and white wine base for this sauce can be used as a starting point for a number of other pasta dishes. You could use tuna, salmon, scallops, calamari or mussels instead of the prawns (shrimp), depending on your mood and what's best at the market on the day. Or use all of the above for a truly decadent seafood marinara.

Cook the pasta in a large saucepan of boiling salted water, following the manufacturer's instructions. Drain and keep warm.

Heat a large frying pan over high heat. Add the butter and oil, then add the onion and sauté for 3–5 minutes, or until translucent.

Add the garlic and prawns and sauté for 1 minute, or until the prawns begin to change colour. Add the tomatoes and chilli and sauté for another minute, or until the tomatoes begin to break down. Season with sea salt and freshly ground pepper.

Pour in the wine, then add the cooked linguine and toss to coat the pasta in the sauce. When the sauce is bubbling and the pasta is heated through, add the basil and toss to combine. Serve drizzled with a little extra virgin olive oil.

MOROCCAN FRIED CHICKEN WITH A DATE AND ORANGE SALAD

Serves 4

Fried chicken

150 g (5½ oz/1 cup) plain
   (all-purpose) flour
3 free-range eggs
100 ml (3½ fl oz) milk
120 g (4¼ oz/2 cups) panko
   breadcrumbs
1 tablespoon ras el hanout
12 chicken tenderloins
olive oil, for frying

Date and orange salad

8 fresh dates, pitted
2 oranges, peeled and segmented
1 fennel bulb, shaved using a
   mandoline
1 handful of wild rocket (arugula)
1 small radicchio, leaves picked
1 small handful of mint leaves, torn
1 tablespoon pomegranate molasses
1 teaspoon dijon mustard
100 ml (3½ fl oz) olive oil
100 g (3½ oz) Marinated feta
   (page 28)

The flavours of this salad will transport you to the markets of Marrakesh. And, instead of chicken, you could try crumbed and fried fish fillets, such as flathead, as a delicious alternative.

TO MAKE THE FRIED CHICKEN, put the flour in a bowl and season with sea salt and freshly ground pepper. In another bowl, whisk together the eggs and milk. In a third bowl, combine the breadcrumbs and ras el hanout.

Dust each chicken tenderloin in the seasoned flour. Dip in the egg mix, allowing the excess to drain off, and then coat with the breadcrumbs.

Place a large heavy-based frying pan over high heat. Pour the olive oil into the pan to a depth of 5 mm (¼ inch). When the oil is hot, add the crumbed chicken in batches and shallow-fry for 3 minutes on each side, or until the chicken is cooked through and the breadcrumbs are golden.

TO MAKE THE DATE AND ORANGE SALAD, combine the dates, orange segments, shaved fennel, rocket, radicchio and mint in a large bowl.

Whisk together the pomegranate molasses, mustard and 1 tablespoon water in a small bowl. Continue whisking while adding the olive oil in a slow, steady stream until combined. Season with salt and pepper. Add the dressing to the salad and toss gently.

To serve, divide the salad among four plates, crumble some feta over the salad and top with the fried chicken. Season with salt and pepper.

SPAGHETTI, ZUCCHINI FLOWERS AND RICOTTA

Serves 4

500 g (1 lb 2 oz) spaghetti
200 g (7 oz) zucchini (courgette)
    flowers
150 ml (5 fl oz) extra virgin olive oil,
    plus extra to serve
4 garlic cloves, finely chopped
1/2 teaspoon chilli flakes
6 anchovy fillets
finely grated zest and juice
    of 1 lemon
10 g (1/4 oz/1/4 cup) finely chopped
    flat-leaf (Italian) parsley
15 g (1/2 oz/1/4 cup) chopped basil
200 g (7 oz) ricotta cheese
lemon wedges, to serve

This is our SoJo version of a classic Italian flavour combination. If you can't get zucchini (courgette) flowers, use julienned zucchini instead.

~~~~~~~~~~~~~~~~~~~~~~~~~~~~~~~~

Cook the spaghetti in a large saucepan of boiling salted water, following the manufacturer's instructions. Drain and keep warm.

Meanwhile, separate the small zucchini from the flowers. Thinly slice the zucchini and tear the flowers into smaller pieces. Set aside.

Heat the olive oil in a large frying pan over medium heat. Add the garlic, chilli and anchovies and cook for 1–2 minutes, without letting the garlic colour too much.

Add the cooked spaghetti to the pan along with the sliced zucchini, torn zucchini flowers, lemon zest, juice and herbs and toss well. Season with sea salt and freshly ground pepper.

Divide among four plates, crumble the ricotta over the top and drizzle with a little extra virgin olive oil. Serve with wedges of lemon to squeeze over.

COLLECTING CURIOS

~~~

I find it's always fun to add a little bit of curiosity to any setting I'm creating, whether that's in the café or at home. I am a collector – some might say a hoarder – and I get a thrill from hunting out quirky objects at thrift shops, garage sales, antique or second-hand dealers... wherever really. I love old vases, children's toys, books, paperweights, boxes, model buildings and old bottles – anything that can add unique interest to a table or sideboard. Sometimes reinventing these knick-knacks with a spray of matt white or black paint can give them a new lease of life.

CHERRY PIE

Serves 12

2 quantities Sweet shortcrust pastry
    (page 68)
180 g (6½ oz) caster (superfine)
    sugar, plus 1 tablespoon extra
3 tablespoons cornflour (cornstarch)
¼ teaspoon salt
1 kg (2 lb 4 oz) whole fresh pitted
    cherries
60 ml (2 fl oz/¼ cup) fresh
    lemon juice
½ teaspoon natural vanilla extract
40 g (1½ oz) unsalted butter, cut
    into 5 mm (¼ inch) cubes
egg wash (1 egg whisked with
    2 tablespoons milk)
icing (confectioners') sugar,
    for dusting
Vanilla ice cream, to serve
    (page 122)

With its lovely, crunchy shortcrust pastry and a filling of the lushest ruby-red fruit, this pie is a real treat when cherries are at their peak in summer. If you need a fix out of season, you can easily use frozen or tinned cherries. We won't tell!

Grease and flour a 28 cm (11 inch) loose-based fluted tart (flan) tin. Roll out half the dough to 5 mm (¼ inch) thick, then roll the dough around the rolling pin, lift and carefully lay it into the tin, gently pressing to fit. Refrigerate for 30 minutes.

Preheat the oven to 220°C (425°F). Roll out the remaining dough to a 30 cm (12 inch) round. Using a large knife or pastry wheel with a fluted edge, cut ten 2 cm (¾ inch) wide strips from the round.

In a bowl, combine the sugar, cornflour and salt. Stir in the pitted cherries, lemon juice and vanilla. Transfer the filling to the pastry-lined tin, mounding the filling slightly in the centre. Dot with the butter.

Arrange the pastry strips on top of the filling to form a lattice. Trim the overhanging pastry strips. Fold the bottom edge of the pastry base up over the ends of the strips and crimp the edges to seal.

Brush the lattice with the egg wash and sprinkle with the extra tablespoon of caster sugar. Place the pie on a baking tray and bake for 15 minutes. Reduce the oven to 180°C (350°F) and bake for a further 45 minutes, or until the filling is bubbling and the crust is golden brown.

Remove the pie from the oven, place on a wire rack and allow to cool completely in the tin. Dust with icing sugar, cut into wedges and serve with vanilla ice cream.

VANILLA ICE CREAM

Makes about 1.25 litres (44 fl oz/5 cups)

500 ml (17 fl oz/2 cups) thickened
   (whipping) cream
500 ml (17 fl oz/2 cups) milk
200 g (7 oz) caster (superfine) sugar
1 vanilla bean
12 egg yolks

COOK'S TIPS

*If freezing overnight, wrap
the ice cream container in a
double layer of plastic wrap.
This will prevent ice crystals
from forming.*

Everyone has their favourite flavour when it comes
to ice cream, but it's just plain old vanilla for me
– especially when you can taste that real vanilla
bean flavour. Home-made ice cream doesn't
require many ingredients and it's actually quite fun
to make. Serve the ice cream on its own, with cakes
and pies, or with poached seasonal fruit.

Pour the cream and milk into a medium heavy-
based saucepan. Add half the sugar.

Slit the vanilla bean down its length with a small
sharp knife. Use the knife to scrape out as many
of the tiny black seeds as you can into the cream
mixture. Cut the vanilla bean into three pieces and
drop it into the pan.

Heat the cream and milk over low heat, stirring
occasionally, until it almost boils. Take the pan off
the heat and set aside so the vanilla can infuse.

Meanwhile, using an electric mixer, whisk together
the egg yolks and the remaining sugar until pale,
thickened and the volume has increased. Add the
cream mixture and beat until well combined.

Return the mixture to the pan and cook over low
heat, stirring constantly until the custard is thick
enough to coat the back of the spoon. Be careful
that it doesn't boil. As soon as you see any bubbles
about to burst to the surface, the custard should be
thick enough; take the saucepan off the heat so
the mixture doesn't curdle. Remove and discard the
pieces of vanilla bean.

Allow the custard to cool completely before
churning in an ice-cream machine following the
manufacturer's instructions. Transfer to a container
and freeze for 4 hours, or until firm (see Cook's
tips). About 20 minutes before serving, transfer
the ice cream to the fridge to soften slightly.

HOT APPLE AND ROSEWATER CIDER

Serves 12

1 large orange, halved
1 teaspoon cloves
2 litres (70 fl oz/8 cups) apple cider
   (or use apple juice)
1 litre (35 fl oz/4 cups) cranberry juice
1 tablespoon honey
3 long cinnamon sticks, about
   10 cm (4 inch)

This spicy, festive beverage is simple to make and gorgeous to serve to friends as the sun sets and day turns to night. You could also add 200 ml (7 fl oz) of brandy... Or more!

~~~~~~~~~~~~~~~~~~~~~~~~~~~~~~~~

Put all of the ingredients in a large saucepan and bring to the boil, stirring constantly. Reduce the heat to low and simmer for 5 minutes.

Remove the pan from the heat and allow to cool to warm – about 65°C (150°F). Strain and serve in heatproof mugs or glasses.

PASSIONFRUIT MELTING MOMENTS

Makes about 12

250 g (9 oz) unsalted butter, softened

1 teaspoon vanilla essence

80 g (2¾ oz/⅔ cup) icing
   (confectioners') sugar, sifted,
   plus extra for dusting

225 g (8 oz/1½ cups) plain
   (all-purpose) flour, sifted

75 g (2½ oz) cornflour (cornstarch),
   sifted

Passionfruit filling

60 g (2¼ oz) unsalted butter,
   softened

pulp of 1 large passionfruit

160 g (5½ oz/1⅓ cups) pure icing
   (confectioners') sugar, sifted

Add passionfruit to the mix and melting moments take on a heavenly new dimension. These are perfect as part of an afternoon tea – serve with a plate of chicken ribbon sandwiches, Raspberry friands (overleaf) and Mimosas (page 20).

Preheat the oven to 160°C (315°F). Line two baking trays with baking paper.

Using an electric mixer, beat the butter, vanilla and sifted icing sugar in a small bowl until light and fluffy. Stir in the combined sifted flours in two batches.

With lightly floured hands, roll half a tablespoon of mixture into a ball. Repeat with the remaining mixture – you should have about 24 balls (aim for an even number). Place the balls on the trays, spacing them about 3 cm (1¼ inches) apart, and flatten slightly with a floured fork.

Bake for about 15 minutes, or until the biscuits are a pale straw colour. Remove from the oven and leave on the trays for 5 minutes before transferring to wire racks to cool.

TO MAKE THE PASSIONFRUIT FILLING, use an electric mixer to beat the butter until light and fluffy. Stir in the passionfruit pulp and icing sugar.

Using a knife, spread the flat side of one biscuit with 1–2 teaspoons of the filling, then top with another biscuit. Repeat with the remaining biscuits and filling. Dust the tops with a little icing sugar.

RASPBERRY FRIANDS WITH CLOTTED CREAM

Makes 12

60 g (2¼ oz) plain (all-purpose) flour
200 g (7 oz) icing (confectioners')
    sugar
120 g (4¼ oz/1¼ cups) almond meal
5 egg whites
180 g (6½ oz) unsalted butter,
    melted
finely grated zest of 1 lemon
24 raspberries
clotted cream, to serve

Friands, fresh from the oven, make the perfect treat for afternoon tea. They are very easy to make and you can double the recipe for the batter – it lasts up to 5 days in the fridge – if you want to bake another batch during the week.

Preheat the oven to 180°C (350°F). Grease a 12-hole friand tray and dust with a little flour, shaking out the excess.

Sift the flour and icing sugar into a large bowl, then stir in the almond meal.

Put the egg whites in a small bowl and lightly whisk with a fork. Add the egg white to the dry ingredients, along with the melted butter and lemon zest, stirring until well combined.

Fill each friand hole two-thirds full, then push two raspberries into each until almost covered by the batter. Bake for 25–35 minutes, until golden and a skewer inserted into the centre comes out clean.

Remove from the oven, leave to cool in the tray for 5 minutes, then turn out onto a wire rack. Serve with clotted cream.

03
—

AUTUMN

AUTUMN BRINGS COLOUR CHANGES, FROM SUMMER GREEN TO VIVID RED AND WARM, BURNT ORANGE

To welcome the new season we carry branches and bunches of foliage into the café, light groups of candles and lamps, stack piles of warm blankets and throws to wrap up in, and bring out all our vintage board games – chess, chequers and backgammon.

Autumn is when we light the wood-burning heater for the first time of the year. With logs cut and stacked against the wall, galvanised tubs filled with kindling and pine cones, and the crackling warmth of the fire, the armchairs near the fireplace are the most coveted locations for breakfast.

Porridge replaces bircher muesli and red wine starts to replace white, as palates change and the days turn colder. Vegetables such as pumpkins, parsnips, carrots and beetroot, and fruit such as pears, apples and figs all make an appearance on the menu. We start to crave heartier foods, bigger portions, warming soups and comfort puddings.

Cosy dinner parties and movie nights are high on the social calendar. Frosty air and brisk walks warm up cold cheeks and get the blood pumping in the morning. Stay warm, people: autumn has arrived!

PEANUT BUTTER MILKSHAKE

Serves 2

140 g (5 oz/½ cup) peanut butter

1 banana

1 tablespoon Easy salted caramel
   sauce (page 70)

2 scoops vanilla ice cream

600 ml (21 fl oz) full-cream
   (whole) milk

We make this with full-cream milk in the café, but you could use low-fat soy or almond milk if you prefer. This shake is very delicious but quite rich, so serve it as a between-meals snack or treat, rather than with a meal.

~~~~~~~~~~

Put all the ingredients into a blender and mix for about 30 seconds, or until the banana is not lumpy and everything is well combined. Pour into two large tall glasses, preferably chilled beforehand in the fridge, and serve.

EARL GREY HOT TODDY

Serves 4

750 ml (26 fl oz/3 cups) water

90 ml (3 fl oz) bourbon whisky

60 ml (2 fl oz/¼ cup) brandy

250 ml (9 fl oz/1 cup) strong earl
   grey tea

2 cinnamon sticks

2 tablespoons honey

1 rosemary sprig

10 juniper berries, crushed

1 orange, washed then roughly
   chopped (including peel)

1 lemon, washed then roughly
   chopped (including peel)

orange and lemon slices, to garnish

This delicious blend of ingredients will warm your hands and cheeks on a cold night. Left to cool to room temperature and then poured over ice, it makes a great summer drink, too.

~~~~~~~~~~

Put all the ingredients, except the orange and lemon garnishes, in a saucepan. Bring to the boil, then turn off the heat. Let the ingredients infuse in the pan for 10 minutes and then strain into a heatproof jug for pouring. Serve in old-fashioned glasses and garnish with the citrus slices.

POACHED QUINCES

Serves 4

2 large quinces
660 g (1 lb 7 oz/3 cups) caster
    (superfine) sugar
2 cinnamon sticks
3 star anise
3 cloves
2 bay leaves
10 black peppercorns
finely grated zest and juice
    of 1 lemon

It does take a while to poach quinces, but your patience will be rewarded with sweet, tender ruby-red quinces that you can add to autumn fruit dishes (page 134), ricotta hotcakes (page 138) or cheese platters. Or roughly chop a few wedges and serve with porridge or bowls of yoghurt. Keep the syrup once all your quinces are gone, reduce it down over heat and drizzle over vanilla ice cream.

~~~~~~~~~~~~~~~~~~~~~~~~

Peel, quarter and remove the cores from the quinces. Reserve the peel and cores.

Put 1.25 litres (44 fl oz/5 cups) water and the remaining ingredients in a large heavy-based saucepan and bring to the boil. Add the quinces and the reserved peel and cores. Cover the surface with a circle of baking paper. Use a plate to keep the quinces submerged. Cover with a lid and simmer for 2–3 hours, or until the quinces are soft and deep pink in colour.

Remove the fruit and set aside. Strain the syrup into a container with a lid, discarding the peel, cores and spices.

Add the quinces to the container with the strained sugar syrup. Cover and store in the fridge for up to 1 week.

AUTUMN FRUIT WITH HONEY YOGHURT

Serves 4

4 green apples, peeled, cut into
    quarters and cored
2 tablespoons light brown sugar
1 cinnamon stick
1 vanilla bean, split in half
    lengthways, seeds scraped
2 tablespoons honey
300 g (10½ oz) plain yoghurt
120 g (4¼ oz) pistachio nuts
400 g (14 oz) Baked pears, cut into
    quarters (page 174)
400 g (14 oz) Poached quinces, cut
    into thick wedges (page 133)
Granola, to serve (optional)
    (page 78)

The colours of the fruit in this dish remind me of autumn leaves as they change from green to yellow, amber to red. Autumn is the time to enjoy warm heady spices and flavours, such as the cinnamon, vanilla bean and honey used here. All the elements of this dish can be prepared in advance and put together at a moment's notice.

Slice the apples lengthways into wedges about 1 cm (½ inch) thick. Place the apples in a large saucepan with 100 ml (3½ fl oz) water, the brown sugar, cinnamon stick, vanilla seeds and bean.

Cover with a lid and gently bring to the boil over medium heat. Reduce the heat to low and simmer for 5–10 minutes, until the fruit is cooked through and soft but not falling apart. Remove from the heat and leave to cool to room temperature. Remove the cinnamon stick and vanilla bean.

In a small mixing bowl, combine the honey and yoghurt. Cover and refrigerate.

Heat a frying pan over low heat, then add the pistachio nuts. Toast them for 5 minutes, stirring often, as they burn very quickly when left unattended. Set aside to cool, then finely chop.

Leave the fruit to cool to room temperature before assembling the dish (or serve the fruit warm or chilled – whatever you prefer). Layer the apples, pears and quinces into four bowls. Top with some honey yoghurt and garnish with the pistachios. If you like, sprinkle some granola over the top.

SEMOLINA PORRIDGE WITH FIGS AND SWEET DUKKAH

Serves 4

Sweet dukkah

50 g (1¾ oz/⅓ cup) pistachio nuts
50 g (1¾ oz/⅓ cup) whole almonds
40 g (1½ oz/¼ cup) hazelnuts
20 g (¾ oz/¼ cup) shredded coconut
70 g (2½ oz/½ cup) sesame seeds
1 teaspoon coriander seeds
1 teaspoon fennel seeds
finely grated zest of 2 oranges
½ teaspoon ground cinnamon
½ teaspoon ground ginger
½ teaspoon ground cardamom
1 tablespoon light brown sugar

Semolina porridge with figs

8 ripe figs
2 tablespoons light brown sugar
1 litre (35 fl oz/4 cups) milk
   or soy milk
180 g (6½ oz) fine semolina flour
2 pinches of ground cinnamon,
   or to taste
1 tablespoon honey, or to taste

Figs have a short season so it's imperative we make the most of them – for breakfast, lunch and dinner.

TO MAKE THE SWEET DUKKAH, put the nuts, coconut, sesame seeds and whole spices in a heavy-based frying pan and toast over medium heat, stirring constantly, until the nuts begin to colour and the spices begin to pop and become fragrant. Tip them out of the pan and allow to cool before transferring to a food processor and pulsing to a coarse crumb consistency. Add the orange zest, ground spices and brown sugar and stir well to combine. Store in an airtight container.

TO MAKE THE SEMOLINA PORRIDGE WITH FIGS, preheat the oven grill (broiler) to medium. Cut the figs in half and dust the cut sides with brown sugar. Place the figs, cut side up, on a baking tray and place under the grill. Cook for about 8 minutes, or until the sugar begins to caramelise and the figs soften. Check on the figs often; if they are already quite soft and ripe, they may only take a few minutes to caramelise.

Heat the milk in a saucepan over low heat and then gradually add the semolina, stirring constantly until all the milk has been absorbed and the semolina has a porridge-like consistency. Add the cinnamon and honey, to taste.

Serve each bowl of semolina porridge topped with four caramelised fig halves and sprinkled with the sweet dukkah.

RICOTTA HOTCAKES WITH POACHED QUINCE AND HONEYCOMB

Serves 4

Honeycomb

335 g (11¾ oz/1½ cups) caster (superfine) sugar

125 ml (4 fl oz/½ cup) honey

2 tablespoons golden syrup or light corn syrup

80 ml (2½ fl oz/⅓ cup) water

2 teaspoons bicarbonate of soda (baking soda)

Ricotta hotcakes

1 kg (2 lb 4 oz) fresh ricotta cheese

500 ml (17 fl oz/2 cups) full-cream (whole) milk

8 free-range eggs, separated

100 g (3½ oz/scant ½ cup) caster (superfine) sugar

400 g (14 oz/2⅔ cups) plain (all-purpose) flour

1 tablespoon baking powder

1 teaspoon sea salt

40 g (1½ oz) butter

12 Poached quince wedges, plus poaching syrup for drizzling (page 133)

Vanilla ice cream, to serve (optional) (page 122)

These ricotta hotcakes have a lovely light, velvety texture and can be paired with any seasonal fruit you fancy. Here they are served with home-made honeycomb, which is very easy and lots of fun to make, but you'll need to invest in a sugar thermometer if you don't already own one.

TO MAKE THE HONEYCOMB, grease and line a baking tray with baking paper. Combine the sugar, honey, golden syrup and water in a saucepan over high heat and bring to the boil. Cook, without stirring, for 5–7 minutes, or until the syrup reaches 154°C (309°F) on a sugar thermometer. Remove from the heat and set aside to allow the bubbles to subside.

Add the bicarbonate of soda and quickly stir with a wooden spoon until combined, being careful as the mixture will foam up. Pour onto the prepared tray and set aside to cool completely. Break into bite-sized pieces and store in an airtight container.

TO MAKE THE RICOTTA HOTCAKES, combine the ricotta, milk, egg yolks and sugar in a large bowl. Sift the flour, baking powder and salt into the wet ingredients, mixing thoroughly. In a clean, dry bowl, whisk the egg whites until firm peaks form, then gently fold them into the batter.

To cook the hotcakes, heat a large heavy-based frying pan over medium heat. Heat a little of the butter until sizzling, then spoon in enough batter to make a 4 cm (1½ inch) round. You should be able to fit three or four hotcakes in the pan at a time. Once bubbles start to form in the batter, flip the hotcakes over and cook the other side for 1 minute. Remove and keep warm. You should get about 12 hotcakes from this quantity of batter.

To serve, put three hotcakes on each plate. Stack three quince wedges on top, drizzle with the poaching syrup and sprinkle with honeycomb. If you like, serve with a scoop of ice cream.

DECORATING WITH FOLIAGE

~~~

Adding foliage to your space can be a clever and
cost-effective way to create great visual impact.
Do remember, however, that leaves and branches
are generally pretty heavy and bulky and so require
large, sturdy vessels to hold them. Another option,
and perhaps a more striking one, is to suspend a
canopy of autumn leaves from the ceiling – all you
need is a few hooks and some strong fishing wire.

Whether your foliage is the bright green of spring
or the gorgeous ambers and reds of autumn, these
displays can look great all year round. At Christmas,
large branches of pine and spruce look wonderfully
festive and smell fantastic, too. You can always add
a string or two of fairy lights – especially overhead
– to increase the sense of drama.

ROAST MUSHROOMS WITH FETA AND BEETROOT RELISH

Serves 4

Autumn is mushroom season, so make the most of the variety on offer. This dish is a café favourite, although many of our customers like to make it an even bigger breakfast by adding a side order of poached eggs.

Beetroot relish

5 rosemary sprigs

2 cloves

peel from 1 orange (be careful not to take too much of the bitter white pith when you peel it)

4 beetroots (beets), scrubbed

125 ml (4 fl oz/½ cup) red wine vinegar

4 tablespoons light brown sugar

2 teaspoons salt

Roast mushrooms

1 kg (2 lb 4 oz) field mushrooms, swiss browns, portobellos or a mixture

4 garlic cloves, thinly sliced

2 tablespoons finely chopped thyme

80 ml (2½ fl oz/⅓ cup) olive oil

8 slices of sourdough

butter, for the toast

100 g (3½ oz) Marinated feta (page 28)

small thyme sprigs, to garnish

TO MAKE THE BEETROOT RELISH, put the rosemary sprigs, cloves and orange peel in a square of muslin (cheesecloth). Wrap up to enclose the ingredients and then secure the bouquet garni with kitchen string. Set aside.

Put the beetroots and 500 ml (17 fl oz/2 cups) water in a saucepan. Bring to the boil, then reduce the heat to low and simmer for 30 minutes, or until the beetroot is tender. Drain the beetroot and set aside to cool. When cool enough to handle, coarsely grate the beetroot onto a plate.

Put the vinegar, brown sugar and salt in the saucepan. Add the grated beetroot and bouquet garni to the pan and bring to the boil, then reduce the heat to low and simmer for 20 minutes, or until most of the liquid has evaporated and the beetroot has caramelised. Set aside to cool. Use the relish immediately or store in an airtight container in the fridge for up to 1 month.

TO MAKE THE ROAST MUSHROOMS, preheat the oven to 180°C (350°F). Put the mushrooms on a baking tray and sprinkle the garlic and thyme over the top. Season well with sea salt and freshly ground pepper and drizzle with the olive oil. Roast for 40 minutes, stirring occasionally.

To serve, toast the sourdough and spread with a little butter. Place two slices of toast on each plate and top with the roast mushrooms. Crumble some feta over the mushrooms and garnish with a few thyme sprigs. Serve with the beetroot relish.

ROAST PUMPKIN OMELETTE WITH PROSCIUTTO AND GOAT'S CHEESE

Serves 4

1 kg (2 lb 4 oz) butternut pumpkin
   (squash)
2 garlic cloves, thinly sliced
1 bird's eye chilli, thinly sliced
½ teaspoon ground cumin
½ teaspoon ground coriander
2 tablespoons olive oil
12 free-range eggs
125 ml (4 fl oz/½ cup) thin
   (pouring) cream
80 g (2¾ oz) butter
1 tablespoon finely chopped sage
1 tablespoon pine nuts, toasted
100 g (3½ oz) goat's cheese
8 slices of prosciutto
1 handful of baby English
   spinach leaves
8 slices of sourdough, toasted
   and buttered

Great for either breakfast or lunch, this omelette combines the rich creaminess of goat's cheese and the earthiness of pumpkin and sage, with just a bit of saltiness from the prosciutto. For a vegetarian meal, simply leave out the prosciutto.

Preheat the oven to 180°C (350°F). Peel the pumpkin and chop it into 2 cm (¾ inch) cubes. Put the pumpkin cubes in a bowl with the garlic, chilli, cumin and coriander. Drizzle with the olive oil, season with sea salt and freshly ground pepper and toss to coat in the oil and seasoning.

Place the pumpkin on a baking tray and roast for 45 minutes, stirring occasionally so it browns all over. Remove from the oven and set aside.

Meanwhile, make the omelettes. Whisk the eggs and cream together in a bowl. Season with salt and pepper.

Melt 20 g (¾ oz) of the butter in an ovenproof, non-stick frying pan over medium heat. Pour a quarter of the egg mixture into the pan, but don't stir until the first signs of setting. At this point, stir gently using a wooden spoon or spatula to push the cooked egg towards the centre of the pan, tilting the pan to allow the uncooked egg to touch the base. When the egg mixture has just set, slide the omelette onto a large baking tray. Repeat to make another three omelettes.

Scatter some roast pumpkin over the omelettes on the tray. Sprinkle with some sage and pine nuts, then crumble some goat's cheese over the top. Place in the oven for 2 minutes to warm through.

Remove from the oven and top each omelette with two slices of prosciutto and some spinach. Fold the omelettes in half, slide onto plates and serve with hot buttered toast.

CAULIFLOWER AND GRUYERE BAKED EGGS

Serves 4

400 g (14 oz) cauliflower, cut into
  small florets
2 garlic cloves, finely chopped
finely grated zest of 1 lemon
1 tablespoon finely chopped thyme
2 tablespoons olive oil
1 small onion, diced
1 teaspoon ground allspice
400 g (14 oz) tin diced tomatoes
150 g (5½ oz/1 cup) fresh or
  frozen peas
3 tablespoons chopped tarragon
4 free-range eggs
100 g (3½ oz) gruyère cheese,
  grated
lemon wedges, to serve
8 slices of sourdough, toasted
  and buttered

Cauliflower and gruyère cheese are one of those flavour combinations that work so well together, just like tomato and basil or figs and blue cheese – there is something magical that happens when these two ingredients come together. The peas and tomato lighten the dish, giving it a little sweetness and acidity.

Preheat the oven to 220°C (425°F). Combine the cauliflower florets, garlic, lemon zest, thyme and 1 tablespoon of the olive oil in a bowl. Season with sea salt and freshly ground pepper. Spread the cauliflower on a large baking tray and roast in the oven for 15–20 minutes, or until golden and tender.

Heat a large saucepan over medium heat. Add the remaining tablespoon of oil, the onion and allspice and sauté for 5–8 minutes, or until the onion begins to brown.

Add the tomatoes to the pan and bring to the boil, then add the roast cauliflower, peas and tarragon and return to the boil. Season with salt and pepper.

Divide the cauliflower mixture among four ovenproof ramekins. Make small dents in the mixture and crack an egg into each hole. Sprinkle with the gruyère.

Reduce the oven to 180°C (350°F). Put the ramekins in the oven and bake for 10–15 minutes, or until the eggs are cooked to your liking. Serve with lemon wedges and hot buttered toast.

MUSHROOM AND LEEK TART

Serves 4

Pastry

280 g (10 oz) plain (all-purpose) flour

140 g (5 oz) chilled butter, cubed

Mushroom and leek filling

25 g (1 oz) butter

1 garlic clove, minced

4 leeks, pale parts only, washed
   well and sliced

250 g (9 oz) field mushrooms, sliced

1 tablespoon chopped thyme

2 free-range eggs

250 ml (9 fl oz/1 cup) thick
   (double/heavy) cream

100 g (3½ oz) parmesan cheese,
   grated

1 small handful of rocket (arugula)
   leaves

1 tablespoon House dressing
   (page 111)

shaved parmesan cheese, to serve

truffle oil, to serve (optional)

This rich, eggy tart is filled with mushrooms and leeks and seasoned with thyme; the truffle oil adds a little extra decadence.

~~~~~~~~~~~~~~~~~~~~~~~~~

TO MAKE THE PASTRY, put the flour and butter in a food processor and pulse until the mixture resembles fine breadcrumbs. Add 8 tablespoons of cold water, 1 tablespoon at a time, pulsing between each addition, until the mixture forms a ball. Tip out onto a work surface and roll into a ball. Cover in plastic wrap and refrigerate for 30 minutes.

Grease and flour four 8 cm (3¼ inch) round tart (flan) tins. Cut the pastry into four portions and roll out each one on a lightly floured surface to a round about 2 cm (¾ inch) larger than the tins. Line the tins with the pastry, cover with plastic wrap and refrigerate for 20 minutes.

Preheat the oven to 200°C (400°F). Line the tart cases with foil and fill with baking beads or dried beans. Place the tins on a baking tray and blind bake for 10 minutes. Remove the foil and beads and bake for a further 5 minutes. Set aside to cool.

TO MAKE THE MUSHROOM AND LEEK FILLING, melt the butter in a large frying pan over medium heat, add the garlic and leek and cook for 10 minutes, stirring occasionally. Add the mushrooms and thyme, season with sea salt and freshly ground pepper, and cook for a further 5 minutes.

Beat the eggs in a large bowl, then gradually add the cream. Stir in the leek and mushroom mixture and half the cheese. Pour the filling into the tart cases and sprinkle with the remaining cheese. Bake for 15–20 minutes, until set and golden brown.

Combine the rocket in a bowl with the dressing. Serve the tarts with the rocket salad and shaved parmesan. If you like, drizzle with a little truffle oil.

SOJO'S TWISTED BENEDICT ON HASH

Serves 4

It's when the best of worlds collide: not really eggs benedict but not eggs florentine either. And it's all served on crispy potato hash and topped off with tarragon-flavoured sauce. Breakfast heaven!

Béarnaise sauce

60 ml (2 fl oz/¼ cup) white wine vinegar
60 ml (2 fl oz/¼ cup) white wine
2 tablespoons minced French shallots
3 tablespoons chopped tarragon
¼ teaspoon sea salt
¼ teaspoon black peppercorns
3 free-range egg yolks
220 g (7¾ oz) clarified butter (see Cook's tips)

Potato hash

1 kg (2 lb 4 oz) all-purpose potatoes, such as sebago, peeled and cut in half
1 free-range egg, lightly beaten
vegetable oil, for frying

200 g (7 oz) shaved leg ham
200 g (7 oz) baby English spinach leaves, sautéed
8 Poached eggs (page 33)

COOK'S TIPS

To clarify the butter, put 250 g (9 oz) butter in a microwave-proof bowl and heat for 1 minute, or until the butter has completely melted. Let the butter sit for 5 minutes and then skim off the salty curd, leaving only the rich, golden liquid. This is the clarified butter.

TO MAKE THE BEARNAISE SAUCE, put the vinegar, white wine, shallots, 1 tablespoon of the tarragon, sea salt and peppercorns in a small saucepan. Bring to the boil and then simmer over medium heat for about 5 minutes, or until the mixture has reduced to a few tablespoons. Remove from the heat and allow to cool slightly.

Transfer to a heatproof bowl placed over a pan of boiling water, ensuring the base of the bowl isn't touching the water. Add the egg yolks and whisk for 5 minutes, or until the mixture begins to thicken. In a slow, steady stream, pour in the clarified butter, whisking as you go. Once all the butter has been incorporated and the sauce has thickened, stir in the remaining tarragon. If the sauce is too thick, add 1 tablespoon of warm water, a little at a time, to thin it. Keep at room temperature until you are ready to serve.

TO MAKE THE POTATO HASH, put the potatoes in a saucepan with 1 teaspoon salt, cover with water and bring to the boil. Simmer for 5 minutes, then drain. When cool enough to handle, julienne the potatoes using a mandoline or food processor (fitted with a julienne disc). Place in a bowl, add the beaten egg and mix well. Season with sea salt and freshly ground pepper. Form the mixture into four large, flat potato 'pancakes'.

Heat the oil in a large heavy-based frying pan over high heat. Cook the potato pancakes in batches for 3 minutes on each side, or until golden and crispy.

Place a potato hash on each plate. Top with some shaved ham, sautéed spinach, two poached eggs and the béarnaise sauce.

STOCK

Any good soup starts with a great stock. We always have at least one soup on our specials' board, and often two – one vegetarian, one meat – in autumn and winter. Some soups are fairly simple and might not have a lot of ingredients, so they have to rely heavily on the stock to give depth of flavour. At home I like to freeze stock in small portions, so I can reheat it quickly when time is short and I want something healthy and nourishing.

CHICKEN STOCK

Makes about 2 litres (70 fl oz/8 cups)

1 whole chicken carcass
1 large carrot, roughly chopped
1 onion, skin on, roughly chopped
1 leek, roughly chopped
3 garlic cloves, roughly chopped
2 celery stalks
6 peppercorns
2 bay leaves
6 parsley stalks
2 thyme sprigs
3 litres (105 fl oz/12 cups) water

Put all the ingredients in a large stockpot and bring to the boil. Reduce the heat to low and simmer for 1 hour. During this time, use a ladle to skim off any impurities that rise to the surface.

Remove from the heat and then strain the liquid into a bowl, pressing on the solids to extract all the flavour. Set aside to cool for about 30 minutes, then place in the fridge. The stock will last for about 1 week in the fridge, but can also be frozen in smaller portions and used as needed.

VEGETABLE STOCK

Makes about 1.5 litres (52 fl oz/6 cups)

The method and ingredients to make vegetable stock are exactly the same as for the chicken stock: simply leave out the chicken and reduce the water content to 2 litres (70 fl oz/8 cups). How easy is that?

CREAM OF MUSHROOM SOUP

Serves 4–6

2 tablespoons olive oil
600 g (1 lb 5 oz) mixed mushrooms,
    sliced
1 onion, diced
2 celery stalks, thinly sliced
3 garlic cloves, minced
1 tablespoon chopped flat-leaf
    (Italian) parsley
1 tablespoon chopped thyme
1.5 litres (52 fl oz/6 cups) Chicken
    stock (page 151)
80 ml (2½ fl oz/⅓ cup) thin
    (pouring) cream
crusty bread, to serve

This warming, comforting soup is ideal for using up any end-of-season mushrooms that are starting to look a little sad. For vegetarian soup, use vegetable stock (page 151) instead of chicken.

Place a large saucepan over medium heat and pour in the olive oil. Add the mushrooms, onion, celery, garlic, parsley and thyme. Stir to combine, then cover with the lid and sweat gently until softened. Spoon 4 tablespoons of mushrooms out of the pan and put to one side.

Pour the stock into the pan and bring to the boil. Reduce the heat to low and simmer for 15 minutes. Season to taste with sea salt and freshly ground pepper, then whiz with a hand-held stick blender until smooth. Pour in the cream and bring just back to the boil, then turn off the heat immediately.

Pour into four bowls and garnish with the reserved mushrooms. Serve with some crusty bread.

LENTIL SOUP WITH PANCETTA AND KALE

Serves 4–6

60 ml (2 fl oz/¼ cup) olive oil
200 g (7 oz) flat pancetta, diced
1 onion, diced
2 carrots, peeled and diced
4 garlic cloves, minced
2 teaspoons ground cumin
2 teaspoons ground coriander
1 teaspoon chopped thyme
¼ teaspoon chilli flakes
1 litre (35 fl oz/4 cups) Chicken
    stock (page 151)
2 x 400 g (14 oz) tins diced
    tomatoes
210 g (7½ oz/1 cup) puy or tiny
    blue-green lentils
300 g (10½ oz/1 cup) chopped kale,
    tough ribs removed
juice of 1 lemon, to taste
crusty bread, to serve

For a vegetarian version of this soup, leave out the pancetta and use vegetable stock (page 151). This recipe is also gluten free.

Warm the olive oil in a large saucepan over medium heat. Add the pancetta, onion and carrots and cook for about 5 minutes, stirring, until the onion is soft and translucent. Add the garlic, cumin, coriander, thyme and chilli.

Pour in a cup of the stock and cook for a few minutes, stirring often. Add the tomatoes, lentils and remaining stock.

Bring the mixture to the boil, then reduce the heat to maintain a gentle simmer. Cook for 30 minutes, or until the lentils are tender but still hold their shape. Add the chopped kale and cook for a further 5 minutes, or until the greens have softened.

Remove the pan from the heat and stir in the lemon juice, to taste. Season with sea salt and freshly ground pepper. Serve with crusty bread.

STEAK SANDWICH WITH CARAMELISED ONION

Serves 4

4 x 150 g (5½ oz) scotch fillets,
   flattened with a meat mallet
2 tablespoons olive oil
4 Turkish pide breads
butter, for the toast
8 tablespoons Beetroot relish
   (page 142)
2 roma (plum) tomatoes, sliced
1 handful of rocket (arugula) leaves
8 slices of Swiss cheese
2 tablespoons horseradish cream
1 quantity Caramelised onions
   (page 104)

After trying many combinations and permutations, this seems to be our customers' favourite mix of fillings for the perfect steak sandwich – although an egg is often a popular addition.

~~~~~~~~~~~~~~~~~~~~~~~~~~~~~~~~~~~~~~

Heat a chargrill pan or heavy-based frying pan over high heat. Season the steaks with sea salt and freshly ground pepper. Add the olive oil to the pan and, when hot, add the steaks and cook for 2 minutes, then turn them over and cook for a further 2 minutes. Allow the meat to rest while you build the rest of the sandwich.

Cut the pide breads in half lengthways. Lightly toast the bread under a grill (broiler) or in a toaster, then butter.

Spread each pide base with 2 tablespoons of beetroot relish, then top with some sliced tomato, rocket, two slices of cheese and a piece of steak. Spread 2 teaspoons of horseradish cream over the bottom of each pide lid and top with some caramelised onions. Put the lids on top, then cut in half to serve.

STYLING WITH PRODUCE

~~~

If you're like me and use a lot of pumpkins (winter squash) in your cooking, why not leave them out on display? If the skin is in good condition and attractive to look at, pumpkins and gourds can last for weeks unrefrigerated and look great stacked together on tables or sideboards. Add a few bowls of chestnuts or walnuts, heaps of candles, some vintage soup tureens, vases and an oil painting or two.

Pomegranates, too, will last for about a week out of the fridge and look fantastic when grouped together in a bowl or on a platter.

The deep reds of the fruit remind me of still life paintings by the great masters, and styled with pewter objects, cut glasses, richly coloured wine and spirit bottles, goblets and such, look really beautiful for autumn.

Set the scene by layering your display. I like to add some leather- and cloth-bound books and big old trays with reflective surfaces to add some shimmer and decadence. Metallics, such as copper, brass and silver, look particularly good with these objects and can add sophistication to your displays.

PULLED PORK BURGER WITH APPLE SLAW

Serves 4

Braised pork neck

1 onion, roughly chopped

1 carrot, roughly chopped

2 celery stalks, roughly chopped

½ bunch thyme

6 bay leaves

1 kg (2 lb 4 oz) pork neck

500 ml (17 fl oz/2 cups) soy sauce

500 ml (17 fl oz/2 cups) Chinese rice wine

125 g (4½ oz/⅔ cup, lightly packed) light
   brown sugar

1 cm (½ inch) knob of fresh ginger, sliced

4 bird's eye chillies, sliced

4 star anise

8 cardamom pods

2 cinnamon sticks

1 tablespoon sichuan peppercorns

1 tablespoon fennel seeds

Apple slaw

2 granny smith apples, julienned

500 g (1 lb 2 oz) Chinese cabbage
   (wong bok), thinly sliced

2 carrots, julienned

1 tablespoon finely chopped dill

1 tablespoon wholegrain mustard

2 tablespoons mayonnaise

1 tablespoon lemon juice

2 firm, ripe avocados

juice of ½ lemon

4 burger buns or brioche rolls

1 handful of mixed lettuce leaves

4 slices of Swiss cheese

4 tablespoons Tomato relish
   (page 49)

Pulled pork is one of the most popular things on the menu at SoJo. Although it's delicious in this burger, the braised pork can also be served as part of an Asian-inspired dinner. Simply remove the pork from the master stock and thinly slice it, then serve on a bed of steamed jasmine rice with some Chinese broccoli (gai larn) and oyster sauce.

TO PREPARE THE BRAISED PORK NECK, preheat the oven to 160°C (315°F). Put the onion, carrot, celery and herbs in a roasting tin or flameproof casserole dish. Place the pork on top. To make a master stock for the pork, combine the soy sauce, rice wine and brown sugar in a bowl, stirring to dissolve the sugar. Add the ginger, chillies, star anise, cardamom, cinnamon, peppercorns and fennel. Pour the liquid and aromatics over the pork, adding water if necessary, so the pork is almost covered in liquid. Cover with baking paper and foil or a lid. Transfer to the oven and cook for 4 hours.

Remove the pork from the stock and place in a bowl. Strain the stock back over the pork and allow to cool in the fridge overnight. Discard the fat from the top of the stock before shredding the pork. Reheat the masterstock, then return the pork to the stock and stir to warm through.

TO MAKE THE APPLE SLAW, combine all the ingredients in a bowl. Season to taste with sea salt and freshly ground pepper.

Cut the avocados in half, remove the stones and then use a spoon to scoop the flesh into a bowl. Add the lemon juice and season with salt and pepper. Use a fork to crush everything together.

Split the buns in half and toast them. Spread the bun bases with crushed avocado, then top with some apple slaw, pulled pork, lettuce and a slice of cheese. Spread the top half of the buns with a spoonful of relish and place on top of the burgers.

BABA GHANOUSH

Makes about 200 g (7 oz)

1 eggplant (aubergine)
1 tablespoon tahini
1 garlic glove, minced
juice of 1 lemon

Keep a bowl of this creamy, smoky eggplant dip in the fridge and serve it with raw vegetables or crusty bread, spread it in a sandwich or serve with grilled meats such as lamb or chicken.

~~~~~~~~~~~~~~~~~~~~~~~~~~~~~~~~~~~~~

Cook the eggplant over the naked flame of a gas stovetop until charred on all sides. Use kitchen tongs to hold the eggplant while you cook it. Alternatively, roast the eggplant over a hot barbecue, or pierce the eggplant all over with a skewer and then roast on a baking tray in a 200°C (400°F) oven, turning occasionally, for 30–40 minutes, or until soft.

Place the charred eggplant in a colander set over a bowl and cover with plastic wrap. Allow to cool. When cool enough to handle, carefully peel off the charred skin with your hands and put the eggplant flesh into the bowl of a food processor.

Add the tahini, garlic and lemon juice and process until smooth. Season with sea salt and freshly ground pepper. Cover and store in the fridge for up to 1 week.

TAHINI YOGHURT DRESSING

Makes about 450 ml (16 fl oz)

200 g (7 oz) plain yoghurt
200 ml (7 fl oz) olive oil
juice of 1 lemon
2 tablespoons tahini
1 small garlic clove, minced

Tahini dressing is used a lot in our kitchens and is great to stir through a potato salad, serve with grilled fish, as a salad dressing or as an alternative to aïoli or mayonnaise.

~~~~~~~~~~~~~~~~~~~~~~~~~~~~~~~~~~~~~

Place all the ingredients in a jug and blend using a hand-held stick blender. Alternatively, process all the ingredients together in a food processor. Season to taste with sea salt and freshly ground pepper. Cover and store in the fridge for up to 5 days.

ROASTED CAULIFLOWER AND BROCCOLI SALAD

Serves 4

250 g (9 oz) cauliflower, cut into
    small florets
250 g (9 oz) broccoli, cut into
    small florets
2 garlic cloves, finely chopped
finely grated zest and juice of
    1 lemon
1 tablespoon finely chopped thyme
100 ml (3½ fl oz) extra virgin olive oil
400 g (14 oz) tin chickpeas, drained
    and rinsed
1 teaspoon smoked paprika
¼ teaspoon chilli flakes
50 g (1¾ oz/⅓ cup) currants
125 ml (4 fl oz/½ cup) hot earl grey tea
200 g (7 oz/1 cup) quinoa
30 g (1 oz/1 cup) roughly torn
    flat-leaf (Italian) parsley
50 g (1¾ oz/1 cup) roughly torn mint
3 spring onions (scallions), thinly sliced
1 tablespoon sherry vinegar
50 g (1¾ oz/⅓ cup) slivered
    almonds, toasted
8 tablespoons Baba ghanoush
    (page 161)
100 g (3½ oz) labne

Roasting the vegetables brings out their flavour and natural sweetness, making this a delicious meal for vegetarians, or a wonderful side salad with lamb, roast chicken or baked salmon. This is easily prepared in advance too, giving you more time with guests or to get on with other things. And if you leave out the labne, this is great for vegans.

Preheat the oven to 220°C (425°F). Combine the cauliflower, broccoli, garlic, lemon zest, thyme and 1 tablespoon of the olive oil in a bowl. Season with sea salt and freshly ground pepper. Spread out on a large baking tray and roast for 15–20 minutes, or until the vegetables are golden and tender.

Pat the chickpeas dry with paper towel, then put them in a bowl. Add the paprika, chilli, 1 tablespoon of the olive oil and season with salt and pepper. Toss to combine. Spread out on a baking tray and roast for 15–20 minutes, or until golden.

Meanwhile, put the currants and earl grey tea in a heatproof bowl. Set aside to soak for 10 minutes, then drain.

Put the quinoa and 375 ml (13 fl oz/1½ cups) salted water in a saucepan over medium heat. Simmer until the water has absorbed, then spread out on a tray to cool slightly.

Combine the parsley, mint, spring onions, vinegar, lemon juice and remaining olive oil in a large bowl. Add the cauliflower, broccoli, chickpeas, quinoa, currants and almonds. Season with salt and pepper and toss to combine.

To serve, spread 2 tablespoons of baba ghanoush onto each plate. Top with the roasted vegetable salad and a spoonful of labne.

LAMB AND COUSCOUS SALAD

Serves 4

4 lamb backstraps or loin fillets
1 tablespoon chopped rosemary
2 garlic gloves, minced
juice of 1 large lemon
2 tablespoons olive oil
500 g (1 lb 2 oz/2⅔ cups) couscous
1 tablespoon ras el hanout
500 ml (17 fl oz/2 cups) boiling water
½ quantity Roast mushrooms
    (page 142)
100 g (3½ oz) wild rocket (arugula)
2 spring onions (scallions), sliced
½ quantity Tahini yoghurt dressing
    (page 161)
100 g (3½ oz) Marinated feta,
    crumbled (page 28)
50 g (1¾ oz) pine nuts, toasted

I remember as a boy eating pine nuts for the first time. My brother had added them to a stuffing mix for roast chicken and it was an absolute taste sensation. This recipe takes its inspiration from Middle Eastern flavours: lamb, feta, lemon and couscous, spiced with earthy ras el hanout and topped with a tahini and yoghurt dressing.

Put the lamb in a bowl with the rosemary, garlic, lemon juice and olive oil. Season with sea salt and freshly ground pepper. Cover and place in the fridge to marinate for at least 2 hours, or overnight.

Put the couscous in a bowl with the ras el hanout, then pour over the boiling water. Mix well and then cover with plastic wrap and leave to cool. Once cool, fluff up the couscous grains using a fork.

Heat a heavy-based frying pan over high heat. Add the marinated lamb and cook for 3 minutes on one side, then turn the lamb over and cook for a further 3 minutes. Remove from the pan and set aside to rest in a warm place for 5 minutes before slicing.

In a large bowl, combine the sliced lamb, couscous, roast mushrooms, rocket, spring onions and tahini yoghurt dressing. Divide among four bowls, then top with the crumbled feta and pine nuts.

ASIAN-STYLE COLESLAW WITH POACHED CHICKEN

Serves 4

Dressing
200 ml (7 fl oz) kecap manis
100 ml (3½ fl oz) sweet chilli sauce
100 ml (3½ fl oz) lime juice

250 g (9 oz) boneless, skinless
   chicken breast fillet
50 g (1¾ oz) tatsoi
400 g (14 oz) Chinese cabbage
   (wong bok), thinly sliced
2 carrots, julienned
2 spring onions (scallions), thinly
   sliced
15 g (½ oz/½ cup) coriander
   (cilantro) leaves
10 g (¼ oz/½ cup) Vietnamese
   mint leaves
100 g (3½ oz/¾ cup) bean sprouts
50 g (1¾ oz/⅓ cup) cashews,
   toasted and roughly chopped
1 teaspoon white sesame seeds,
   toasted
1 teaspoon black sesame seeds,
   toasted
2 tablespoons fried shallots
lime wedges, to serve

Perfect for a sunny autumn Sunday lunch with friends, this salad is quick and easy – it can be made in advance and dressed just before serving. With its lovely fresh flavours and crunchy texture, this is one of SoJo's best sellers.

TO MAKE THE DRESSING, put the kecap manis, sweet chilli sauce and lime juice in a glass jar. Put the lid on and shake to combine. Any left-over dressing can be kept in the fridge for up to 1 week.

Put the chicken in a deep frying pan. Cover with water and bring to a gentle simmer over medium heat. Reduce the heat to low and poach the chicken for 5–8 minutes. Turn the heat off and leave the chicken to cool in the liquid.

Thinly slice or shred the poached chicken and place in a large bowl. Add the tatsoi, cabbage, carrots, spring onions and herbs. Add 200 ml (7 fl oz) of the dressing and toss to combine.

Divide the salad among four bowls and top with the bean sprouts, cashews, sesame seeds and fried shallots. Serve with a wedge of lime.

MUSHROOM RISOTTO WITH GORGONZOLA

Serves 4

50 g (1¾ oz) dried porcini mushrooms
1.5 litres (52 fl oz/6 cups) Chicken
    stock (page 151)
2 tablespoons olive oil
1 small onion, finely diced
1 small leek, pale part only, washed
    well and finely diced
2 celery stalks, finely diced
1 teaspoon minced garlic
330 g (11½ oz/1½ cups) arborio rice
½ quantity Roast mushrooms
    (page 142)
40 g (1½ oz) butter
2 tablespoons chopped flat-leaf
    (Italian) parsley
2 tablespoons chopped thyme
50 g (1¾ oz/½ cup) finely grated
    parmesan cheese
100 g (3½ oz) gorgonzola or other
    blue cheese
1 tablespoon vincotto (see Cook's tips)

COOK'S TIPS

*Vincotto, meaning 'cooked wine',
is a sweet–sour condiment used
in both sweet and savoury
cooking – as a salad dressing,
drizzled over fish, or over
desserts such as panna cotta.
It is available from specialist
Italian delicatessens and
gourmet food stores.*

This risotto combines dried porcini mushrooms with an assortment of roasted field mushrooms (page 142). You can use whatever mushrooms are in season, but keep an eye out especially for slippery jacks and saffron-coloured pine mushrooms.

Put the dried mushrooms in a bowl, cover with 250 ml (9 fl oz/1 cup) water and set aside to soak for 1 hour. Drain the mushrooms, discarding the soaking liquid, then roughly chop.

Bring the stock to the boil in a saucepan, then reduce the heat to low and keep at a simmer.

Heat the olive oil in a large heavy-based saucepan over medium heat. Add the onion, leek, celery and garlic and sauté for about 5 minutes, or until translucent. Add the porcini and sauté for a further 5 minutes. Add the rice and stir for a minute or two until well coated with the onion mixture.

Add the hot stock, a cupful at a time, stirring constantly until each cup of stock has been absorbed before adding another. Once you've added 4 cups of the stock, stir in the roast mushrooms and another cup of stock. When the stock has absorbed, check if the rice is al dente. You may want to add a little more stock depending on your taste.

Stir in the butter, herbs and parmesan, and season with sea salt and freshly ground pepper. Divide the risotto among four bowls, crumble over the gorgonzola and drizzle with the vincotto.

PAPPARDELLE WITH DUCK RAGU

Serves 4

2 tablespoons olive oil

4 duck marylands (leg quarters)

1 carrot, finely chopped

1 celery stalk, finely chopped

1 onion, finely chopped

4 garlic cloves, finely chopped

2 teaspoons fennel seeds, ground

250 ml (9 fl oz/1 cup) red wine

1 orange, zest removed in strips
   with a potato peeler

1 cinnamon stick

500 ml (17 fl oz/2 cups) Chicken
   stock or Vegetable stock
   (page 151)

400 g (14 oz) tin crushed tomatoes

500 g (1 lb 2 oz) pappardelle pasta

2 tablespoons chopped flat-leaf
   (Italian) parsley

4 tablespoons finely grated
   pecorino cheese

This is a rich and satisfying dish, perfect with a glass of pinot noir. If you can source fresh pasta, your guests will love you even more.

Heat the olive oil in a large heavy-based saucepan or flameproof casserole dish over medium heat. Working in two batches, add the duck marylands and cook, turning once, for 6–8 minutes until golden. Remove from the pan and set aside.

Add the carrot, celery, onion and garlic and cook, stirring occasionally, for 6–8 minutes until tender.

Add the fennel and stir to combine, then return all the duck to the pan. Add the wine, strips of orange zest and cinnamon stick and bring to a simmer. Add the stock and tomatoes and return to a simmer, then reduce the heat to low and simmer for $1\frac{1}{2}$–2 hours, or until the duck is tender.

Remove the duck from the pan and set aside to cool. When cool enough to handle, shred the meat, discarding the bones. Return the shredded duck meat to the pan over low heat, stir to combine, and season with sea salt and freshly ground pepper. Cover and keep warm.

Meanwhile, cook the pappardelle in a saucepan of boiling salted water following the manufacturer's instructions. Drain well, add to the ragu (in batches if all the pasta doesn't fit in your pan) and toss to combine. Sprinkle with the parsley and pecorino before serving.

GRILLED FISH WITH ASIAN GREENS AND MISO BUTTER

Serves 4

Miso butter

4 tablespoons butter, at room
    temperature
2 tablespoons white miso paste
freshly ground sichuan pepper
    (optional)

4 x 150 g (5½ oz) blue-eye
    trevalla (or cod) fillets
3 tablespoons olive oil
400 g (14 oz) Chinese broccoli
    (gai larn)
2 garlic cloves, minced
½ tablespoon thinly sliced
    fresh ginger
4 spring onions (scallions),
    thinly sliced
1 tablespoon sesame oil
2 tablespoons oyster sauce
1 tablespoon soy sauce
2 pinches of sugar
juice of 1 lime

For this recipe I've used Chinese broccoli with the blue-eye, however bok choy (pak choy), mustard greens, water spinach (ong choy) or amaranth leaves are all great seasonal variations – as is wild barramundi, which is at its best in late summer.

TO MAKE THE MISO BUTTER, mash the butter and miso together using a fork. If you like, season with sichuan pepper. Roll the miso butter into a log, cover in plastic wrap and refrigerate until needed. Any left-over butter can be frozen for another day.

Season the fish with sea salt and freshly ground pepper. Heat a chargrill pan or heavy-based frying pan over medium heat, and add 2 tablespoons of the olive oil. Put the fish, skin side down, in the hot pan and cook for 5 minutes, then turn and cook for a further 3 minutes. Remove from the pan and rest in a warm place for 5 minutes.

Bring a large saucepan of salted water to the boil. Plunge the Chinese broccoli into the boiling water and cook for about 1½ minutes until just tender, then remove and drain well.

Heat a large wok or saucepan over high heat. Add the remaining olive oil, the garlic and ginger and cook for about 30 seconds, or until aromatic. Add the spring onions, sesame oil, oyster sauce, soy sauce, sugar and lime juice. Season with salt and pepper, then add the Chinese broccoli and toss to coat in the sauce. Stir-fry for a further 2–3 minutes.

To serve, divide the stir-fried greens among four plates. Top with the fish and a slice of miso butter.

AUTUMN FIREWOOD

~~~

If you are lucky enough to have a wood-burning fire,
pizza oven, brazier or the like, have fun with your wood
storage. Neatly stacked logs of timber with bunches
of bound sticks for kindling, big baskets of pine cones
and even timber offcuts can look very effective and
rustic when displayed with precision and abundance.
I particularly like seeing these stacked in hand-made,
firm-sided raffia or jute bags, or even piled up in
vintage wooden fruit crates. Keep your old newspapers
and matches out of sight in an old wooden or steel
box, and invest in a great set of fire tongs.

PEAR TARTE TATIN

Serves 4

Baked pears

4 small pears

110 g (3¾ oz/½ cup) caster
    (superfine) sugar

20 g (¾ oz) unsalted butter

1 vanilla bean, halved lengthways
    and seeds scraped

2 tablespoons brandy

100 g (3½ oz) caster (superfine) sugar

100 ml (3½ fl oz) brandy

1 vanilla bean, halved lengthways
    and seeds scraped

50 g (1¾ oz) unsalted butter, cubed

1 sheet ready-rolled puff pastry

cream or ice cream, to serve

Here's another French classic that has made it onto our favourites list at SoJo. A traditional tarte tatin is made with apples, but I've gone for pears here, although poached quinces (page 133) would work wonderfully too. You could, of course, use apples – my favourites are granny smiths.

~~~~~~

TO MAKE THE BAKED PEARS, preheat the oven to 160°C (315°F). Butter an ovenproof dish that will fit the pears snugly.

Peel, quarter and core the pears. Arrange the pears in the dish. Sprinkle the sugar over the pears, then dot with a little butter and some of the vanilla seeds. Pour in the brandy and cover with baking paper and foil. Bake for 1½–2 hours, or until the pears are soft and light golden brown. Remove and set aside.

Increase the oven to 190°C (375°F). You will need an ovenproof frying pan to cook the tart. Put the pan over medium heat and add the sugar, brandy, vanilla seeds and bean. Let the sugar dissolve and cook until the mixture forms a light caramel.

Add the baked pears, arranging them neatly in the pan, and cook for about 5 minutes, shaking the pan gently to make sure the pears aren't catching on the base. Dot with the cubed butter, then lay the pastry over the top. Using a wooden spoon, tuck the pastry edge down around the pears, taking care not to touch the caramel, as it is very hot.

Bake for 25–30 minutes, or until the pastry is golden and the caramel is bubbling up around the edge. Remove from the oven.

Get a serving plate that is larger than your pan and put the plate on top of the pan. Using oven gloves to protect your hands, invert the pan onto the plate. Allow the caramel to cool slightly before serving with cream or ice cream.

APPLE AND CINNAMON TEACAKE

Serves 8–10

2 free-range eggs, separated
165 g (5¾ oz/¾ cup) caster
 (superfine) sugar
180 ml (6 fl oz) milk
45 g (1½ oz) unsalted butter, melted
½ teaspoon natural vanilla extract
225 g (8 oz/1½ cups) self-raising
 flour, sifted
1 apple, peeled, cored and sliced

Cinnamon topping
1 tablespoon caster (superfine)
 sugar
½ teaspoon ground cinnamon
10 g (¼ oz) unsalted butter, melted

There is something about the smell of cinnamon that is evocative of cooler weather for me. Maybe it reminds me of my grandmother, who always seemed to be baking teacakes as soon as the weather 'turned'.

Preheat the oven to 190°C (375°F). Lightly grease a 20 cm (8 inch) round cake tin.

Using an electric mixer, beat the egg whites until firm peaks form. Add the sugar, 1 tablespoon at a time, beating constantly until the mixture is thick and glossy. Beat in the egg yolks.

Combine the milk, melted butter and vanilla in a jug. Using a large metal spoon, gently fold the sifted flour alternately with the milk mixture into the beaten eggs.

Pour into the prepared cake tin and arrange the apple slices on top. Bake for 30–35 minutes, or until a skewer inserted into the centre of the cake comes out clean.

TO MAKE THE CINNAMON TOPPING, combine the sugar and cinnamon in a bowl. Brush the hot cake with melted butter and sprinkle with the cinnamon sugar. Serve warm.

CLASSIC CHOCOLATE BROWNIES

Makes 15

125 g (4½ oz) unsalted butter
300 g (10½ oz) caster (superfine)
    sugar
70 g (2½ oz) unsweetened cocoa
    powder
3 eggs
150 g (5½ oz/1 cup) plain
    (all-purpose) flour
1 teaspoon baking powder
150 g (5½ oz/1 cup) white
    chocolate melts (buttons)
icing (confectioners') sugar,
    for dusting (optional)

This has got to be one of the easiest – and yummiest – brownie recipes ever. We have customers who buy whole trays to take back to work. We presume they are going to share...

Preheat the oven to 160°C (315°F). Grease and line a 20 x 30 cm (8 x 12 inch) shallow baking tin.

Melt the butter in a small saucepan over medium heat or in a microwave. Combine the sugar and cocoa powder in a large mixing bowl. Add the melted butter and mix well. Add the eggs and mix well.

Sift in the flour and baking powder and stir to combine, then fold in the white chocolate melts. Spread the brownie mixture into the tin, smoothing the top.

Bake for 30–40 minutes, or until just set and a skewer inserted into the middle of the brownie comes out almost clean. The outside of the brownie should be firm and cooked through, but the middle should still be slightly moist – the brownie will continue to cook for 5 minutes or so as it cools, so take care not to overcook it.

Leave the brownies to cool in the tin before turning out onto a wire rack. Cut into small squares and dust with icing sugar if you like.

04
—

WINTER

WINTER: WE SOMETIMES FIND OURSELVES WANTING TO STAY INDOORS AND HIBERNATE. IF ONLY WE COULD... LIFE IS BUSY.

I think it's important to embrace winter in all its glory. The skies might be grey, cloudy and intense and the temperatures may plummet, but I always find there is something romantic about this season. The idea of staying inside, rugging up and keeping warm, and even just slowing down a bit, is all very appealing to me. OK, yes, it's cold. And grey. And wet. And sometimes windy. So, wear warm clothes and keep a collapsible umbrella with you at all times; that's my advice. (Truth be known, I do get excited about a midwinter sunshine getaway though!)

In the café we dim the lighting to 'moody' and enjoy the flames of the fire as they flicker and reflect in the glass firebox. We add rich, deep colours and luxurious textures: woollen throws and hides; colourful artworks in vibrant plums, pinks and crimsons; rustic platters of lemons and bowls of artichokes; flickering candles in brass candlesticks... you get the picture.

Food tends to be richer and more robust both in colour and flavour. Potatoes, carrots, leeks, turnips and beetroots begin to appear on the menu, along with silverbeet, spinach and cabbage. Meats are roasted, braised and slow cooked; fruits are stewed and poached. What a glorious time of year for food!

HARVEST MULLED WINE

Makes about 1 litre (35 fl oz/4 cups)

150 g (5½ oz/heaped ⅔ cup) sugar
12 small oranges, cut in half
750 ml (26 fl oz) bottle red wine
250 ml (9 fl oz/1 cup) cranberry juice
125 ml (4 fl oz/½ cup) brandy
4 cinnamon sticks
2 teaspoons allspice berries
4 star anise
1 teaspoon whole cloves
10 lightly crushed cardamom pods
1 vanilla bean, cut in half
   lengthways
½ teaspoon freshly grated nutmeg
10 rosemary sprigs

When it's cold outside and friends are coming over, there's nothing better than a glass of mulled wine to warm things up. You don't need to shell out on an expensive bottle of wine either – a moderately priced bottle will do the trick. And feel free to experiment a little: use dark rum instead of brandy, or add some crushed juniper berries or lime zest.

~~~~~~~~~~~~~~~~~~~~~~~~

Put 250 ml (9 fl oz/1 cup) water and the sugar in a crockpot or large heavy-based saucepan and place over high heat. Stir to dissolve the sugar. Juice eight of the oranges and add the juice to the pot.

Add the remaining ingredients and heat just until the liquid comes to a simmer. Reduce the heat to as low as possible and let it sit on the heat for 10 minutes. Strain and serve in heatproof glasses.

BAKED APPLE PORRIDGE

Serves 4

Baked apples

4 large green apples, such as
   granny smiths
45 g (1½ oz/¼ cup, lightly packed)
   light brown sugar
1 teaspoon ground cinnamon
80 g (2¾ oz/½ cup) chopped
   dates
60 g (2¼ oz/¼ cup) chopped
   walnuts
20 g (¾ oz) butter, softened
125 ml (4 fl oz/½ cup) boiling water

Porridge

190 g (6¾ oz/2 cups) rolled
   (porridge) oats
500 ml (17 fl oz/2 cups) milk
¼ teaspoon sea salt
extra cold milk, to serve

This baked apple and oat mixture will warm the cockles of your heart on a cold winter's morning. It's almost like having dessert for breakfast!

TO **MAKE THE BAKED APPLES**, preheat the oven to 190°C (375°F). Cut the apples into quarters and remove the cores. Put the apples in a baking dish, skin side down.

Combine the brown sugar, cinnamon, dates and walnuts in a small bowl. Scatter the sugar and date mixture over the apples and then dot with the butter. Carefully pour the boiling water into the dish, to avoid wetting the apple topping. Bake for 30–45 minutes, until the apples are cooked through and tender.

TO **MAKE THE PORRIDGE**, put the oats in a saucepan with the milk and 1 litre (35 fl oz/4 cups) water. Slowly bring to the boil over high heat, stirring frequently. Reduce the heat to low, add the salt and simmer, stirring regularly, for about 10 minutes, until it has the consistency you like. Remove from the heat, cover the pan and leave for 5 minutes.

Spoon the porridge into four bowls and serve topped with the baked apples, dates and walnuts. Serve with extra milk on the side.

FRENCH TOAST WITH MAPLE BACON, BANANA AND PECANS

Serves 4

Maple bacon

8 bacon rashers

2 tablespoons pure maple syrup, plus extra to serve

French toast

4 free-range eggs

80 ml (2½ fl oz/⅓ cup) milk

80 ml (2½ fl oz/⅓ cup) thin (pouring) cream

30 g (1 oz) butter

8 thick slices of crusty white bread

2 bananas, sliced

60 g (2¼ oz/½ cup) chopped pecans

Take weekend French toast to the next level with this delicious, crispy maple-glazed bacon.

TO MAKE THE MAPLE BACON, preheat the oven to 200°C (400°F). Line a baking tray with baking paper. Arrange the bacon in a single layer on the tray. Bake for about 15 minutes, or until the fat is rendered and the bacon is beginning to brown. Brush the bacon with the maple syrup and bake for a further 5 minutes, or until the bacon is browned and sticky. Transfer to a wire rack to drain. Keep warm.

TO MAKE THE FRENCH TOAST, whisk together the eggs, milk and cream in a bowl. Melt half the butter in a large non-stick frying pan over medium heat. Dip four slices of bread, one at a time, in the egg mixture until soaked, then drain off the excess.

Fry the bread for 2 minutes on each side, or until golden brown. Remove from the pan and keep warm while you cook the remaining slices.

To serve, stack two pieces of French toast on each plate. Top with half a sliced banana, two slices of maple bacon and some pecans. Drizzle with a little maple syrup.

SAUTEED PINE MUSHROOMS WITH HUMMUS AND DUKKAH

Serves 4

Pistachio dukkah

100 g (3½ oz/⅔ cup) sesame seeds
50 g (1¾ oz) whole almonds
50 g (1¾ oz/⅓ cup) hazelnuts
100 g (3½ oz/⅔ cup) pistachio nuts
50 g (1¾ oz) cumin seeds
50 g (1¾ oz) coriander seeds
50 g (1¾ oz) fennel seeds

Hummus

400 g (14 oz) tin chickpeas,
   drained and rinsed
1 tablespoon tahini
1 tablespoon lemon juice
1 garlic clove, roughly chopped

Mushrooms

100 g (3½ oz) butter
1 garlic clove, minced
400 g (14 oz) pine mushrooms, sliced
1 tablespoon chopped sage
1 tablespoon sour cream
8 slices of sourdough, toasted
   and buttered

Dukkah is a very versatile spice mix that adds a touch of the exotic to simple dishes such as grilled fish or vegetables. Use a good-quality ready-made dukkah if you don't have time to make your own.

TO MAKE THE PISTACHIO DUKKAH, preheat the oven to 180°C (350°F). Put the sesame seeds on a baking tray and roast until golden brown, watching them carefully as they can easily burn. Roast the almonds and hazelnuts separately for 4–5 minutes, until brown. Tip the hazelnuts into a tea towel and rub off as many of the skins as you can.

Put the pistachios, almonds and hazelnuts in a food processor and blitz until roughly crushed, being careful not to turn them into dust. Transfer the nuts and sesame seeds to a mixing bowl.

Heat a non-stick frying pan over medium heat. Add the cumin, coriander and fennel seeds and stir constantly until the seeds start to pop and become aromatic. Blend in a spice grinder or finely crush in a mortar and pestle. Add the spices to the nut mixture, mix well and then season with sea salt and freshly ground pepper. Store the dukkah in an airtight container for up to 1 month.

TO MAKE THE HUMMUS, put all the ingredients in a food processor. Process until roughly combined. With the motor running, add some water, a little at a time, until you have achieved the desired consistency. Season with salt and pepper.

TO COOK THE MUSHROOMS, heat a frying pan over medium–high heat. Add the butter, garlic and mushrooms and sauté until the mushrooms are soft. Stir in the sage and sour cream and season to taste with salt and pepper.

To serve, spread the buttered toast with some hummus. Top with the mushrooms and sprinkle with a few tablespoons of the pistachio dukkah.

POACHED EGGS WITH CHORIZO AND OLIVE RAGU

Serves 4

Chorizo and olive ragu

2 tablespoons olive oil

1 small onion, finely diced

400 g (14 oz) chorizo sausage, each
    sliced diagonally into 5 pieces

250 ml (9 fl oz/1 cup) white wine

400 g (14 oz) tin diced tomatoes

1 tablespoon dried basil

2 bay leaves

20 pitted kalamata olives

8 free-range eggs

1 quantity hollandaise sauce
    (use the recipe for Béarnaise
    sauce, page 148, leaving out
    the tarragon)

1 small handful of basil leaves

8 slices of sourdough, toasted
    and buttered

I invented this dish quite by accident when cooking a weekend breakfast for a group of friends. It has since made its way onto SoJo's menu and subsequently has become a bit of a signature dish for the café. Now we simply cannot change or take it off the menu!

〜〜〜〜〜〜〜〜〜〜〜〜〜〜

TO MAKE THE CHORIZO AND OLIVE RAGU, heat the olive oil in a saucepan over high heat and sauté the onion for about 5 minutes, or until translucent. Add the chorizo and cook until browned. Deglaze the pan with the wine, stirring well, then add the tomatoes, basil and bay leaves.

Bring to the boil, then reduce the heat to low and add the olives. Simmer for about 15 minutes, or until the mixture is thick and the tomatoes are a deep, rich red colour. Season with sea salt and freshly ground pepper. Set aside and keep warm. This ragu can be cooked the day before.

To serve, poach the eggs for 2–4 minutes in a pan of simmering water (page 33).

Divide the chorizo ragu among four bowls, then top with two poached eggs and a generous tablespoon of hollandaise sauce. Scatter with basil and serve with buttered toast.

COFFEE

~~~

My home town of Melbourne has a borderline
obsession with all things coffee. However, 30 years
ago, when I was just starting my career, things were
a little different. Back then, my friends and I thought
a cappuccino was pretty flash – so much so that we
would often drive over 30 minutes to Lygon Street in
multicultural Carlton, just to have a cup, or possibly
two, and play the jukebox. That makes me sound
about 100 years old, I know!

At home now I use a French press to make my coffee.
I have two sizes: a two-cup, because there's usually
me and someone else; and a six-cup, for when friends
come over.

Classic percolators do a great job too, but the most
important ingredient is the coffee – freshly ground from
a good supplier is always going to make a superior
brew. Change it up occasionally with different blends
and single origins. Or try a shot of coffee over ice, with
or without milk.

SCRAMBLED EGGS WITH SWISS BROWNS, SILVERBEET AND TRUFFLE OIL

Serves 4

500 g (1 lb 2 oz) silverbeet
   (Swiss chard)
150 g (5½ oz) butter
1 garlic clove, minced
400 g (14 oz) Swiss brown
   mushrooms, sliced
1 tablespoon chopped thyme
8 free-range eggs
80 ml (2½ fl oz/⅓ cup) thin
   (pouring) cream
8 slices of sourdough, toasted
   and buttered
shaved parmesan cheese,
   to serve
truffle oil, to serve

The combination of scrambled eggs, parmesan and truffle is a classic, and we've also thrown in some silverbeet to make it all appear healthier! A word of warning: a few drops of truffle oil goes a very long way, so use it sparingly – or not at all. I tend to put it on the table and let everyone add their own.

Trim the silverbeet leaves off the central stalks, discarding the stalks. Place the leaves in a sink filled with cold water and wash well to remove the dirt. Remove from the water, rinse under running water and drain. Pat dry thoroughly, then chop the leaves and set aside.

Heat a non-stick frying pan over medium–high heat. Add 50 g (1¾ oz) of the butter and, when melted, add the garlic, mushrooms and thyme and cook for about 5 minutes, or until the mushrooms have softened. Season with sea salt and freshly ground pepper. Transfer to a baking tin and keep warm in a 120°C (235°F) oven.

Clean out the pan and return it to medium–high heat. Melt another 50 g (1¾ oz) of butter and sauté the silverbeet until wilted. Keep warm.

Whisk the eggs and cream together in a bowl. Season with salt and pepper. Return the frying pan to medium heat and add the remaining 50 g (1¾ oz) of butter. When the butter begins to sizzle, pour the egg mixture into the pan. Don't stir until the first signs of setting. When the egg starts to set, stir gently using a wooden spoon or spatula to push the cooked egg towards the centre of the pan, tilting the pan to allow the uncooked egg to touch the base. Cook for 2 minutes, or until the eggs are just set.

Place two pieces of buttered toast on each plate and top with the scrambled eggs. Place the mushrooms and silverbeet on the side. Sprinkle with shaved parmesan and drizzle with truffle oil.

BAKED BEANS WITH HAM HOCK AND EGGS

Serves 4

Cooking with beans is a sensational way to add more nutrients, such as fibre and protein, to your diet and it's a very cost-effective way to feed a lot of people. For a vegetarian meal, simply leave out the ham hock.

Baked beans

375 g (13 oz) dried cannellini beans, soaked in cold water overnight

1 ham hock

1 large onion, diced

2 carrots, diced

3 capsicums (peppers), diced

400 g (14 oz) tin diced tomatoes

3 garlic cloves, minced

2 bay leaves

1 tablespoon chopped thyme

1 teaspoon smoked paprika

1 teaspoon ground cumin

1 teaspoon ground coriander

100 ml (3½ fl oz) pure maple syrup

---

8 free-range eggs

100 g (3½ oz) baby English spinach leaves

40 g (1½ oz) butter

100 g (3½ oz) goat's cheese

4 slices of sourdough, toasted and buttered

TO MAKE THE BAKED BEANS, preheat the oven to 160°C (315°F). Put the drained beans and ham hock in a flameproof casserole dish or baking dish. Add the onion, carrots, capsicums, tomatoes, garlic, bay leaves, thyme and spices and mix together. Pour in enough water to cover by 5 cm (2 inches). Seal the dish with a tight-fitting lid or with a piece of baking paper and then foil.

Bake for 2 hours, then remove the dish from the oven and give everything a stir. Check the water level and top it up if it's getting too dry. Return to the oven and cook for a further 2 hours, or until the beans are tender and the sauce is rich and thick.

Remove the hock and allow to cool. When cool enough to handle, shred the meat from the bones and return the meat to the beans. Place the casserole dish (or transfer the meat and beans to a saucepan) on the stovetop over medium heat and stir to combine everything and warm through. Stir in the maple syrup and season with sea salt and freshly ground pepper.

To serve, poach the eggs for 2–4 minutes in a pan of simmering water (page 33). Place another frying pan over medium heat and sauté the spinach in the butter until lightly wilted.

Place a large spoonful of baked beans on each plate, then top with some sautéed spinach and two poached eggs. Crumble some goat's cheese over the top and serve with buttered toast.

SAUERKRAUT

Fills a 1 litre (35 fl oz/4 cup) glass jar

1.4 kg (3 lb 2 oz) green cabbage
1½ tablespoons sea salt
1 tablespoon caraway seeds

COOK'S TIPS

● *The sauerkraut should be ready after 3 days, but you can leave it to continue fermenting for 10 days or even longer.*
● *Any scum should be skimmed off the top either during the fermentation period or before refrigerating.*
● *If you see any mould, skim it off immediately and make sure your cabbage is fully submerged under the liquid.*

It's not difficult to make your own sauerkraut and it can be kept for up to 2 months in the fridge.

Discard the limp outer cabbage leaves, reserving one of the larger leaves. Cut the cabbage into quarters and trim out the core. Slice each quarter down its length to make eight wedges. Slice each wedge crossways into very thin ribbons. Place in a large bowl and sprinkle with the sea salt and caraway seeds. Work the salt into the cabbage by massaging and squeezing the cabbage with your hands. This will take 5–10 minutes; the cabbage will become limp and start to release some of its liquid.

Pack the cabbage into a 1 litre (35 fl oz/4 cup) glass jar or non-reactive container. Every so often, tamp down the cabbage with your fist. Pour the liquid released by the cabbage (after massaging it) into the jar. To keep the cabbage submerged in its liquid, place the reserved cabbage leaf on top. Place a smaller jar into the mouth of the jar and weigh it down with clean stones or marbles. Cover with muslin (cheesecloth) and secure with a rubber band. This allows air to flow in and out of the jar, but prevents dust or insects from getting in.

Over the next 24 hours, use the smaller jar to press down on the cabbage every so often. The cabbage will soften and release its liquid, and the liquid will rise over the top of the cabbage. If this hasn't occurred after 24 hours, dissolve 1 teaspoon salt in 250 ml (9 fl oz/1 cup) water and add enough to submerge the cabbage.

As the cabbage is fermenting, keep it away from direct sunlight and at a cool room temperature – ideally 18–24°C (64–75°F). Check it daily and press the cabbage down if it is floating above the liquid. Start tasting the sauerkraut after 3 days. When it tastes good to you, remove the weight, screw the lid on the jar and refrigerate.

OPEN REUBEN MELT

Serves 4

Russian dressing
185 ml (6 fl oz/³/4 cup) Aïoli
    (page 111)
60 ml (2 fl oz/¹/4 cup) tomato sauce
1 tablespoon horseradish
1 teaspoon sriracha hot chilli sauce
1 teaspoon worcestershire sauce
¹/4 teaspoon sweet paprika
sea salt, to taste

8 slices of rye sourdough
butter, for the toast
400 g (14 oz) Sauerkraut (page 197
    or deli-bought)
400 g (14 oz) thinly sliced pastrami
    or corned beef
8 slices of Swiss cheese

You can use deli-bought sauerkraut for your Reuben melt, but we have included a recipe (page 197) if you want to try making it at home. It takes about 3 days for the cabbage to ferment, so plan ahead of time.

~~~~~~~~~~~~~~~~~~~~~~~

TO MAKE THE RUSSIAN DRESSING, whisk all the ingredients together in a small bowl. Cover and set aside.

Heat an oven grill (broiler) or salamander to medium. Lightly toast and butter the sourdough. Place the toast on a baking tray, top with some sauerkraut, pastrami, a dollop of Russian dressing and then finish with the cheese. Grill (broil) until the cheese has melted and the sandwich is warmed through. Serve immediately.

BUBBLE AND SQUEAK WITH FRIED EGGS AND CAPONATA

Serves 4

Caponata

185 ml (6 fl oz/¾ cup) olive oil

2 eggplants (aubergines), diced

1 onion, sliced

4 celery stalks, diced

2 teaspoons salt

80 g (2¾ oz/½ cup) pitted green
  olives

80 g (2¾ oz/½ cup) drained
  capers

400 g (14 oz) tin crushed tomatoes

170 ml (5½ fl oz/⅔ cup) white wine
  vinegar

1 tablespoon sugar

Bubble and squeak

1 quantity Caramelised onions
  (page 104)

3 cupfuls of mashed potato

2 cupfuls of cooked kale

4 tablespoons plain (all-purpose)
  flour

50 g (1¾ oz/½ cup) grated
  gruyère cheese

1 free-range egg, lightly whisked

80 ml (2½ fl oz/⅓ cup) olive oil

8 lamb and fennel sausages

8 slices of haloumi

80 ml (2½ fl oz/⅓ cup) olive oil

20 g (¾ oz) butter

8 free-range eggs

Here, all the usual elements of a classic 'fry-up' are given a Mediterranean twist with the haloumi, lamb and fennel sausages, and eggplant caponata.

TO MAKE THE CAPONATA, heat 125 ml (4 fl oz/½ cup) of the olive oil in a large frying pan over medium heat. Add the eggplants, onion, celery and salt and fry gently for 10 minutes. Add the remaining oil and the remaining ingredients and bring to the boil. Reduce the heat and simmer for 10 minutes, stirring occasionally. Use the caponata immediately or cool to room temperature and store in an airtight container in the fridge for up to 2 weeks.

TO MAKE THE BUBBLE AND SQUEAK, mix together the caramelised onions, mashed potato, kale, flour, cheese and egg in a large bowl. Season with sea salt and freshly ground pepper.

Heat 2 tablespoons of the olive oil in a large non-stick frying pan over medium heat. Add 80 ml (2½ fl oz/⅓ cup) of mixture to the pan, flattening it into a roundish fritter shape about 1 cm (½ inch) thick. Cook for 2–3 minutes on each side until golden brown. Keep warm in a 120°C (235°F) oven. Repeat with the remaining batter – you should get about eight fritters.

Next, cook the sausages in the same pan. Remove and keep warm. Fry the haloumi on both sides until golden brown (add a little more oil to the pan if needed). Drain on paper towel.

To fry the eggs, heat half the olive oil and half the butter in the pan over high heat. Add four eggs and fry until the whites are opaque and the edges are crisp (page 32). Repeat with the remaining oil, butter and eggs.

To serve, place two fritters on each plate and top each one with a slice of grilled haloumi and a fried egg. Serve with the sausages and caponata.

LAMB SHANK AND PEARL BARLEY SOUP

Serves 4–6

2 tablespoons olive oil
4 lamb shanks, trimmed
1 large onion, diced
4 garlic cloves, minced
1 carrot, diced
2 celery stalks, diced
2 litres (70 fl oz/8 cups) Chicken
  stock (page 151)
100 g (3½ oz/½ cup) pearl barley
2 tablespoons chopped rosemary
1 tablespoon chopped flat-leaf
  (Italian) parsley
finely grated zest of 1 lemon

Warming and comforting, this hearty soup is the perfect weeknight meal-in-a bowl. Any leftovers can be frozen, then reheated for a quick meal or supper when you're feeling lazy or in a rush.

~~~~~~~~~~~~~~~~~~~~~~~~~~~~~~~~~~~~~~

Heat the olive oil in a large saucepan or flameproof casserole dish over high heat and brown the lamb shanks in two batches. Remove and set aside.

Add the onion, garlic, carrot and celery to the pan and cook for 5 minutes, or until lightly browned.

Return the shanks to the pan and add the stock, barley and rosemary. Bring to the boil, then reduce the heat to low, cover and simmer for 2 hours. Remove the shanks and cool slightly. When cool enough to handle, take the meat off the bone and flake into pieces.

Return the meat to the soup in the pan over low heat. Stir in the parsley and lemon zest and season to taste with sea salt and freshly ground pepper before serving.

CHORIZO, KIDNEY BEAN AND SWEET POTATO SOUP

Serves 4–6

2 tablespoons olive oil
1 onion, diced
400 g (14 oz) chorizo sausage,
   roughly chopped
2 bay leaves
1 tablespoon chopped thyme
1 teaspoon ground allspice
½ teaspoon chilli flakes
400 g (14 oz) tin diced tomatoes
400 g (14 oz) tin kidney beans,
   rinsed and drained
1 large sweet potato, diced
2 litres (70 fl oz/8 cups) Chicken
   stock or Vegetable stock
   (page 151)
small thyme sprigs, to garnish
4–6 tablespoons sour cream
   (optional)

Here's another winter soup that is a meal in itself. There really is nothing better than curling up in front of the fire with a bowl of warm soup, some crusty bread and a glass of Aussie tempranillo.

Heat the olive oil in a large saucepan over high heat and sauté the onion for about 5 minutes, or until translucent. Add the chorizo and cook until it starts to brown. Add the herbs, spices, tomatoes, kidney beans, sweet potato and stock.

Bring to the boil, then reduce the heat and simmer for 20–30 minutes, until the sweet potato is tender. Season with sea salt and freshly ground pepper. Serve garnished with a few thyme sprigs and perhaps a tablespoon of sour cream.

TOMATO, FENNEL AND SALMON SOUP WITH SAFFRON AIOLI

Serves 4–6

Bouquet garni

1 orange, zest removed in strips
   with a potato peeler
1 cinnamon stick
4 star anise
1 teaspoon fennel seeds
1 teaspoon coriander seeds
1 teaspoon black peppercorns
6 bay leaves
6 thyme sprigs

Soup

2 tablespoons olive oil
1 onion, sliced
1 fennel bulb, thinly sliced
2 garlic cloves, minced
¼ teaspoon chilli flakes
250 ml (9 fl oz/1 cup) white wine
2 x 400 g (14 oz) tins diced
   tomatoes
1 litre (35 fl oz/4 cups) Chicken
   stock or Vegetable stock
   (page 151)
300 g (10½ oz) skinless salmon
   fillet, diced
a small pinch of saffron threads

Saffron aïoli

a pinch of saffron threads
½ quantity Aïoli (page 111)

Inspired by bouillabaisse, this is a hearty and comforting soup, heady with the aroma of saffron. Throw in some mussels and prawns (shrimp) and you have a delicious seafood stew.

TO MAKE THE BOUQUET GARNI, tie all the ingredients together in a piece of muslin (cheesecloth).

TO MAKE THE SOUP, heat the olive oil in a large saucepan over medium heat. Add the onion, fennel, garlic and chilli and sauté for about 7 minutes, or until the onion and fennel are translucent and starting to colour.

Add the wine, tomatoes, stock, salmon, saffron and bouquet garni. Bring to the boil, then reduce the heat to low and simmer for 20 minutes. Season with sea salt and freshly ground pepper.

TO MAKE THE SAFFRON AIOLI, put the saffron in a small bowl with 1 tablespoon water and leave to soak for 15–20 minutes, to activate the stamen and release the colour. Drain, discarding the water. Add the saffron to the aïoli and mix well.

To serve, ladle the soup into bowls and top with a dollop of saffron aïoli.

CROQUE MONSIEUR

Serves 4

200 ml (7 fl oz) milk

2 thyme sprigs

1 bay leaf

4 peppercorns

1 garlic clove, crushed

20 g (¾ oz) butter, plus extra for buttering the bread

20 g (¾ oz) plain (all-purpose) flour

200 g (7 oz/2 cups) grated gruyère cheese

freshly grated nutmeg (optional)

8 slices of sourdough

4 teaspoons dijon mustard

8 slices of leg ham

Make sure you use the best quality ham and gruyère cheese for these famous French 'toasties', as the quality of the ingredients is what makes these sandwiches shine. To turn this into a croque madame, top your toasted sandwich with a fried egg, served sunny side up.

Pour the milk into a saucepan and add the thyme sprigs, bay leaf, peppercorns and garlic. Bring to the boil, then remove from the heat and set aside for 10 minutes to allow the flavours to develop.

Melt the butter in a small saucepan over high heat. Add the flour and cook for 1–2 minutes, until the roux is foaming and golden.

Gradually whisk in the strained milk, a little at a time, until smooth. Continue whisking for a further 3–4 minutes, until the sauce thickens. Remove the pan from the heat and stir in half the cheese until melted. Grate in a little nutmeg, if using, and season with sea salt and freshly ground pepper.

Spread four slices of sourdough with the mustard, then top each one with two slices of ham and a quarter of the remaining cheese. Spread the remaining slices of bread with 1 tablespoon of the cheese sauce and close the sandwich.

Spread the sandwiches with a little butter. Toast on a flat grill or in a frying pan or sandwich press until golden and crispy on the outside and oozing cheesy goodness on the inside.

LAYING THE TABLE

~~~

Setting a beautiful table is more about style than spending a fortune. Sometimes food presented on the simplest white plates can look the most effective. The best white plates I have found are from hospitality dinnerware supply shops. Often they are commercial-grade ceramic too, which makes them very durable. These suppliers usually stock good-quality, inexpensive stainless-steel cutlery as well, or you could try finding something vintage on eBay or at a local market.

Lately I have also been buying hand-made ceramics from local artisans. These stoneware vessels can look fantastic on the table, especially for serving soups and rustic-style dishes.

Using vintage china that is inexpensive but stylish can set the scene for a classic breakfast or brunch. Play with colour palettes that reflect the seasons and highlight the produce you are serving. When buying vintage crockery, bear in mind that it will need to be hand washed rather than going in the dishwasher.

It's also fun to mix and match your glassware. I tend to gravitate towards clear glass mainly because I prefer the aesthetic, but I also like the idea of serving orange juice in a wine glass or wine in a tumbler and, once again, collecting vintage glasses from second-hand shops.

HEIRLOOM CARROTS WITH GRAIN SALAD AND PRESERVED LEMON YOGHURT

Serves 4

60 g (2¼ oz) butter

2 tablespoons honey

6 thyme sprigs

8 heirloom carrots (use a mix of colours)

2 parsnips

1 garlic bulb, separated into cloves, peeled

Grain salad

95 g (3¼ oz/½ cup) wild black rice

100 g (3½ oz/½ cup) quinoa

100 g (3½ oz/½ cup) puy or tiny blue-green lentils

90 g (3¼ oz/½ cup) freekeh

40 g (1½ oz/¼ cup) currants

125 ml (4 fl oz/½ cup) hot earl grey tea

35 g (1¼ oz/¼ cup) slivered almonds

1 tablespoon sunflower seeds

1 tablespoon pepitas (pumpkin seeds)

1 tablespoon linseeds (flaxseeds)

15 g (½ oz/¼ cup) chopped flat-leaf (Italian) parsley

15 g (½ oz/¼ cup) chopped mint

2 spring onions (scallions), thinly sliced

juice of 1 lemon

80 ml (2½ fl oz/⅓ cup) extra virgin olive oil

Preserved lemon yoghurt

260 g (9¼ oz/1 cup) Greek-style yoghurt

1 tablespoon finely chopped preserved lemon rind (page 56)

1 tablespoon honey

With colours ranging from deep yellow to crimson and purple, heirloom carrots are a feast for the eyes. Here they are served with a salad of mixed ancient grains, which, on its own, would make a wonderful accompaniment for grilled meat and fish. Look out for heirloom carrots at your local farmer's market.

Preheat the oven to 200°C (400°F). Line a roasting tin with baking paper.

Melt the butter in a small saucepan over low heat, then stir in the honey and thyme sprigs. Peel the carrots and parsnips and cut in half diagonally (or leave whole if small). Put the vegetables and garlic cloves in a bowl, drizzle with the butter mixture and toss to coat. Transfer to the tin and season with sea salt and freshly ground pepper. Roast the vegetables and garlic for 35–40 minutes, or until tender, turning them occasionally.

TO MAKE THE GRAIN SALAD, boil the wild rice, quinoa, lentils and freekeh separately in salted water until just cooked. Drain well and allow to cool. Soak the currants in the hot tea for 10 minutes, then drain.

Place a heavy-based frying pan over medium heat. Add the almonds and toss until lightly toasted. Tip into a bowl. Add the sunflower seeds, pepitas and linseeds to the pan and toss gently until the seeds are evenly coloured. Remove to a separate bowl.

Combine the cooked grains in a large bowl with the toasted almonds, currants, parsley, mint, spring onions, lemon juice and olive oil. Season to taste.

TO MAKE THE PRESERVED LEMON YOGHURT, combine all the ingredients in a small bowl.

To serve, divide the grain salad among four plates. Top with the roast vegetables, preserved lemon yoghurt and sprinkle with the toasted seeds.

CONFIT DUCK WITH BEETROOT AND ORANGE SALAD

Serves 4

Confit duck

315 g (11 oz/1 cup) rock salt
1 tablespoon juniper berries
1 teaspoon fennel seeds
1 teaspoon coriander seeds
1 teaspoon black peppercorns
6 star anise
1 small handful of thyme sprigs,
   tough stalks removed
4 garlic cloves, peeled
4 duck marylands (leg quarters)
1 litre (35 fl oz/4 cups) duck fat

Beetroot and orange salad

1 large beetroot (beet), unpeeled and
   trimmed, but left with a short stalk
1 tablespoon olive oil
1 teaspoon balsamic vinegar
1 orange, peeled and segmented
1 fennel bulb, shaved using a
   mandoline
2 witlof (chicory)
1 small handful of watercress sprigs
100 ml (3½ fl oz) House dressing
   (page 111)

Duck confit is one of my favourite dishes. A confit is any type of food, often duck or pork, that has been salted, then cooked and preserved in its own fat.

~~~~~~~~~~~~~~~~~~~~~~~~~~~~~~~~~~~~~

TO PREPARE THE CONFIT DUCK, put all the ingredients, except the duck marylands and fat, in a food processor and pulse until well combined. Put the marylands in a large bowl and toss with the salt mix. Lay the marylands in a non-reactive container, cover and refrigerate overnight. Wipe off the salt mix and pat dry with paper towel.

Preheat the oven to 120°C (235°F). Place the duck in a baking tin. Melt the duck fat in a saucepan and pour over the duck. Cover with baking paper and foil and cook for 1–1½ hours, or until the meat is just falling off the bone. Let the duck cool in the fat for 10 minutes, then transfer the duck to a container. Before the fat congeals, strain the fat over the duck using a fine mesh strainer. Cover and refrigerate.

TO MAKE THE BEETROOT AND ORANGE SALAD, cook the beetroot in boiling salted water for 45 minutes, until tender. Drain and cool. Preheat the oven to 190°C (375°F). Rub the skin off the beetroot (wear rubber gloves) and cut into wedges. Toss with the olive oil and balsamic vinegar and season. Place in a baking dish and roast for 30–40 minutes, until starting to caramelise. Keep warm.

Toss all the remaining salad ingredients in a bowl with the dressing. Add the beetroot just before serving, so it doesn't stain the other ingredients.

To serve, remove the duck pieces from the container (briefly warm the duck in the microwave to soften the fat). Heat a heavy-based frying pan over high heat. Add the duck, skin side down, and cook for 5 minutes, or until the skin is crispy and golden. Place in the oven for 10 minutes to warm through. Serve the beetroot and orange salad topped with a warmed duck maryland.

PAPPARDELLE WITH BEEF CHEEK RAGU AND GREMOLATA

Serves 4

Beef cheek ragu

1 kg (2 lb 4 oz) beef cheeks,
    trimmed
100 ml (3½ fl oz) olive oil
1 large onion, diced
1 carrot, diced
2 celery stalks, diced
4 garlic cloves, minced
750 ml (26 fl oz/3 cups) red wine
500 ml (17 fl oz/2 cups) Chicken
    stock (page 151)
400 g (14 oz) tin diced tomatoes
1 small handful of thyme sprigs,
    tied together
1 small handful of rosemary sprigs,
    tied together
2 bay leaves
2 cinnamon sticks

Gremolata

20 g (¾ oz/1 cup) flat-leaf (Italian)
    parsley leaves
1 garlic clove, minced
finely grated zest of 2 lemons

400 g (14 oz) pappardelle pasta
shaved parmesan cheese, to serve

Slow-braised beef cheek produces the most lip-smacking, sticky and unctuous sauce, ideal for pappardelle but equally delicious with soft polenta.

TO MAKE THE BEEF CHEEK RAGU, preheat the oven to 150°C (300°F). Season the beef cheeks with sea salt and freshly ground pepper.

Heat the olive oil in a casserole dish over medium– high heat. Add the beef cheeks and seal all over for 10 minutes, or until browned. Remove and set aside.

Add the onion, carrot, celery and garlic to the hot dish and cook over low heat for about 15 minutes, or until the vegetables have softened. Deglaze the dish using 250 ml (9 fl oz/1 cup) of the red wine and allow the wine to reduce by half.

Return the beef to the dish along with the stock, tomatoes, thyme, rosemary, bay leaves, cinnamon sticks and remaining wine. Bring to a simmer for 5 minutes, then remove from the stovetop. Cover with the lid or baking paper and foil and transfer to the oven. Cook for 2 hours, or until the meat is very tender.

Using two forks, gently shred the beef into smaller pieces. Remove the herb bunches and season the ragu with salt and pepper. Keep warm in a 120°C (235°F) oven.

TO MAKE THE GREMOLATA, put the parsley, garlic and lemon zest on a chopping board and finely chop the parsley, incorporating the garlic and zest until everything is well combined.

To serve, cook the pappardelle in a saucepan of boiling salted water following the manufacturer's instructions. Drain the pasta, add the ragu and toss to combine. Serve topped with the gremolata and shaved parmesan.

PENNE WITH PORK AND VEAL SAUSAGE RAGU

Serves 4

600 g (1 lb 5 oz) Italian-style pork
   and veal sausages
100 ml (3½ fl oz) olive oil
1 small onion, diced
3 garlic cloves, minced
¼ teaspoon chilli flakes
250 ml (9 fl oz/1 cup) red wine
400 g (14 oz) tin diced tomatoes
500 ml (17 fl oz/2 cups) Chicken
   stock (page 151)
400 g (14 oz) penne
100 g (3½ oz) ricotta salata, shaved
   (see Cook's tips)

COOK'S TIPS

Ricotta salata is a type of hard ricotta that has been pressed and then salted and dried. It can be shaved or grated over pasta, salads, or you could serve it on sliced new-season tomatoes, with a drizzle of good olive oil and some sea salt and freshly ground pepper.

You can use any Italian sausage for this recipe – we sometimes use pork and wine or pork and fennel – though look for a sausage with a good marbling of fat throughout. Although this recipe has some fairly sophisticated flavours, it's by far our most popular kids' pasta dish – just be careful that you don't add too much chilli, if any.

Remove the sausages from their skins and cut the meat into bite-sized pieces.

Heat the olive oil in a large frying pan over medium–high heat. Add the onion and sauté for 5 minutes, or until translucent. Add the sausage pieces, garlic and chilli and cook for 2–3 minutes, until beginning to brown.

Pour in the red wine and bring to the boil, then continue to boil until reduced by half. Add the tomatoes and stock and return to the boil, then reduce the heat to low and simmer for 10 minutes. Season with sea salt and freshly ground pepper.

Meanwhile, cook the penne in a saucepan of boiling salted water following the manufacturer's instructions. Drain the pasta, add the ragu and toss to combine. Serve topped with the ricotta salata.

SCALLOP, ROASTED FENNEL AND LEMON RISOTTO

Serves 4

4 baby fennel bulbs
80 ml (2½ fl oz/⅓ cup) olive oil
1.5 litres (52 fl oz/6 cups) Vegetable stock (page 151)
1 small onion, finely diced
1 small leek, pale part only, finely diced
2 celery stalks, finely diced
1 teaspoon minced garlic
330 g (11½ oz/1½ cups) arborio rice
40 g (1½ oz) butter
1 tablespoon chopped dill
1 tablespoon chopped flat-leaf (Italian) parsley
1 teaspoon finely grated lemon zest
12 scallops, roe removed if preferred
extra virgin olive oil, to serve

I love scallops and fennel and lemon, so put them all together in this lovely creamy risotto and I'm in foodie heaven. For an impressive start to a dinner party, serve a little of the risotto in a scallop shell and arrange a scallop on top.

Preheat the oven to 190°C (375°F). Cut each fennel bulb into eight wedges, reserving some fronds for garnish. Toss the fennel with 2 tablespoons of the olive oil and season with sea salt and freshly ground pepper. Place the fennel in a single layer in a baking tin and roast for 30–40 minutes, or until tender. Remove from the oven and keep warm.

Meanwhile, to make the risotto, bring the stock to the boil in a saucepan, then reduce the heat to low and keep at a simmer.

Heat the remaining olive oil in a large heavy-based saucepan over medium heat. Add the onion, leek, celery and garlic and sauté for about 5 minutes, or until translucent. Add the rice and stir for a minute or two until well coated with the onion mixture.

Add the hot stock, a cupful at a time, stirring constantly until each cup of stock has been absorbed before adding another. Once you've added 4 cups of the stock, add the roast fennel and another cup of stock. When the stock has absorbed, check if the rice is al dente. You may want to add a little more stock depending on your taste. Stir in the butter, herbs and lemon zest and season with salt and pepper.

Just before the risotto is ready, cook the scallops. Heat a heavy-based frying pan over high heat. Add the scallops and cook for 30 seconds on each side, or until golden and just cooked through.

Serve the risotto topped with the scallops and garnished with the reserved fennel fronds. Drizzle with a little extra virgin olive oil.

COQ AU VIN

Serves 4

1.6 kg (3 lb 8 oz) whole chicken,
    cut into 8 pieces
12 French shallots, peeled
1 large carrot, diced
2 celery stalks, diced
1 small garlic bulb, separated into
    cloves, peeled
2 bay leaves
1 small handful of parsley stalks,
    tied together
1 small handful of thyme sprigs,
    tied together
750 ml (26 fl oz/3 cups) red wine
2 tablespoons olive oil, plus extra
    if needed
150 g (5½ oz) flat pancetta, diced
200 g (7 oz) Swiss brown
    mushrooms, quartered
125 ml (4 fl oz/½ cup) Chicken
    stock (page 151)

If you are time poor you could skip the first step of this recipe, but marinating the chicken overnight will give your coq au vin a greater depth of flavour.

Put the chicken pieces in a large mixing bowl along with the shallots, carrot, celery, garlic cloves, herbs and red wine. Cover and place in the fridge to marinate overnight.

Heat a large flameproof casserole dish over medium heat. Add the olive oil and sauté the pancetta for 5 minutes, or until brown, then remove from the dish. Sauté the mushrooms for 5 minutes, then remove from the dish.

Remove the chicken from the marinade and strain the marinade into a bowl, reserving the liquid and vegetables separately. Working in batches, add the chicken pieces to the casserole dish and brown them for about 10 minutes, adding a little extra oil if needed, to prevent the chicken from sticking to the dish. Remove and set aside. Add the reserved vegetables and herbs and sauté over medium heat for about 15 minutes, or until softened.

Return the chicken, pancetta and mushrooms to the dish. Pour in the reserved marinade and the stock and bring to the boil. Boil for 5 minutes, reduce the heat to low and simmer, stirring occasionally, for 30 minutes. Season with sea salt and freshly ground pepper.

Preheat the oven to 160°C (315°F). Place the dish in the oven and cook for 1 hour, or until the chicken is tender. Remove the bay leaves and bunches of parsley and thyme. Serve with creamy mashed potato and a green salad.

CANDLELIGHT

〜〜〜

A few years ago I travelled to London and went to a pizza restaurant in Brick Lane for lunch. It was winter and, even though it was only around 1 pm, the whole restaurant was lit up with dozens of candles. It was the first time I had seen this style of lighting during the day and I thought it was really beautiful.

In Melbourne when it's dark and cold, we have an open fire in the café and light plenty of candles to create a warm, cosy ambience. You can easily create this type of atmosphere at home and it is relatively inexpensive. The key to getting it right is to use lots of candles – select all different shapes and sizes, but I think it's most successful when you only use white wax. I also place candles in glass vases, not only for safety reasons, but because it reflects the light better around the room and makes the space look more sophisticated.

I have also mixed real wax candles with some very authentic looking, battery-operated flickering light candles, bought online. They last for ages and are very effective, especially if the idea of a naked flame at home or at work concerns you. The trick is to keep the fake candles up high, so you don't give away your secret. I won't tell if you don't.

DATE AND BANANA LOAF
Serves 10

150 g (5½ oz) chopped,
    pitted dried dates
200 g (7 oz) light brown sugar
300 g (10½ oz/2 cups) self-raising
    flour
260 g (9¼ oz) mashed ripe banana
    (2 large bananas)
60 g (2¼ oz/½ cup) chopped
    walnuts
½ teaspoon bicarbonate of soda
    (baking soda)

Sweet and sticky with dates and bananas, this loaf is perfect for a cold winter afternoon. Cut it into thick slices and serve warm with a knob of butter, perhaps some honey, and a cup of earl grey tea.

Preheat the oven to 180°C (350°F). Lightly grease a 14 x 21 cm (5½ x 8¼ inch) loaf (bar) tin and line the base and sides with baking paper.

Put the dates and brown sugar in a saucepan over low heat. Add 250 ml (9 fl oz/1 cup) water and cook, stirring, for 2 minutes, or until the sugar has dissolved. Increase the heat to medium and bring to the boil for 2 minutes. Remove from the heat.

Add the flour, mashed banana, walnuts and bicarbonate of soda to the pan and stir until combined. Spoon the mixture into the prepared tin. Smooth the surface with the back of the spoon.

Bake for 40 minutes, or until a skewer inserted into the centre of the loaf comes out clean. Set aside for 5 minutes to cool in the tin before turning out onto a wire rack. Slice and serve warm or at room temperature, with butter and honey.

FLOURLESS CHOCOLATE CAKE

Serves 12

250 g (9 oz) dark chocolate melts
   (buttons)
250 g (9 oz) unsalted butter, chopped
250 g (9 oz/2½ cups) almond meal
20 ml (½ fl oz) espresso coffee
8 free-range eggs
250 g (9 oz) caster (superfine) sugar
½ teaspoon sea salt
icing (confectioners') sugar,
   for dusting
thick (double/heavy) cream,
   to serve

This cake uses almond meal instead of flour –
perfect for anyone who is gluten intolerant or
simply avoiding wheat.

Preheat the oven to 160°C (315°F). Grease a 23 cm
(9 inch) spring-form tin and line with baking paper.

Melt the chocolate and butter in a heatproof bowl
over a pan of simmering water, ensuring the base
of the bowl isn't touching the water. Stir until
smooth, remove the bowl and leave to cool a little.
Stir in the almond meal and coffee.

Using an electric mixer, whisk the eggs, sugar and
salt for about 5 minutes, or until doubled in volume.
Gently fold into the melted chocolate mixture.

Pour into the tin and bake for 40–50 minutes, until
just set on top. Place the tin on a wire rack to cool.
Dust with icing sugar and serve with cream.

SPICED CHAI

Makes about 1 litre (35 fl oz/4 cups)

1 litre (35 fl oz/4 cups) good-quality
   soy milk
200 ml (7 fl oz) water
2 tablespoons English breakfast
   tea leaves
10 green cardamom pods
10 whole black peppercorns
1 teaspoon fennel seeds
2 cinnamon sticks
2 star anise
1 teaspoon freshly ground nutmeg
1 small knob (20 g/¾ oz) fresh
   ginger, thinly sliced
honey, to taste (I use 2 tablespoons)

My choice of milk is soy, but use full-cream (whole)
or almond milk if you prefer (I find the spices are
too overpowering for low-fat milk though). In
summer, I leave this to cool and then pour it over
vanilla ice cream and ice – a sort of chai affogato.

Put all the ingredients, except the honey, in a
saucepan and bring to the boil over high heat.
Reduce the heat to low and simmer gently, stirring
occasionally, for 30 minutes. Remove the pan from
the heat and add honey, to taste.

Let the chai cool for 5 minutes and then strain
through a fine mesh strainer. Discard the waste.
Pour into a teapot and serve. The chai can also be
stored in the fridge for up to 5 days; simply reheat
it on the stove when needed.

MARMALADE AND GRANOLA SLICE

Makes 15 pieces

90 g (3¼ oz) unsalted butter,
    softened
110 g (3¾ oz/½ cup) caster
    (superfine) sugar
2 free-range eggs
100 g (3½ oz/⅔ cup) plain
    (all-purpose) flour, sifted
50 g (1¾ oz/⅓ cup) self-raising
    flour, sifted
340 g (12 oz) orange marmalade
60 g (2¼ oz/¼ cup) glacé ginger,
    finely chopped
200 g (7 oz) Granola (page 78)
icing (confectioners') sugar,
    for dusting (optional)

Any jam will work in this slice, but I just love the tartness of a good marmalade.

Preheat the oven to 160°C (315°F). Lightly grease a 20 x 30 cm (8 x 12 inch) cake tin and line the base and sides with baking paper.

Using an electric mixer, beat the butter, sugar and 1 egg in a small bowl until light and fluffy. Stir in the sifted flours. Spread the dough into the prepared tin. Combine the marmalade and ginger in a small bowl and then dot the marmalade over the dough.

Using a fork, lightly whisk the remaining egg in a bowl. Add the granola and stir to combine. Spread the granola mixture over the marmalade.

Bake for about 40 minutes, or until a skewer inserted into the centre of the slice comes out clean. Allow to cool in the tin. Dust with icing sugar if desired and cut into squares.

INDEX

233

ACKNOWLEDGEMENTS

~~~

Firstly, I would like to thank my chef, Matthew Palmer. Without his incredible talent and passion this cookbook would have been much more difficult to write. Working with Matt has been a joy and an inspiration, so I thank him from the bottom of my heart.

I would also like to acknowledge the hard work and dedication of the kitchen and front of house staff at South of Johnston and Oxford Larder. You all make work an absolute pleasure.

To my family, who have been there throughout, to staff members and colleagues over the years, to the glorious customers I have had the pleasure of getting to know, to my mentors in the industry and to the friends who have heard nearly ALL my stories, I say a big thank you.

None of this would have been possible without the love and support of my partner, Simon Carver. It's always nice to shut away the world at home and relax with someone so understanding and generous, who unfailingly has my best interests at heart. And Fergus, my staffy, who appears on a few pages (undoubtedly looking for food dropped during the shoot).

This is the first time I have been asked to embark on an endeavour such as this, but, my oh my, what a team I had: Armelle, Deb, Corinne, Matt, Jane, Madeleine and Kim... Thanks for everything; it has been amazing. Cheers everyone and get cooking!

The publisher and author would like to thank the following artists whose work appears in the pages of All Day Café:
Page 6, Gregor Kregar (neon sculpture)
Page 14–15, left to right, Simon Carver, Paul McKenzie, Fiona Hall, Kirby
Page 27, Laura Skerlj
Page 52, left to right, Clive Stratford, Simon Carver, Paul McKenzie
Page 136, Annika Koops
Page 173, Graham Miller
Page 182–3, Graham Miller, Laura Skerlj
Page 229, Robert Doble and Simon Strong, Laura Skerlj, Gregor Kregar, Shane Thoms
Page 236–7, Ivan Goodacre, Stephen Bird (ceramic plate), Timothy Belcher, JF Lagace, Datsun Tran

Published in 2017 by Murdoch Books, an imprint of Allen & Unwin

Murdoch Books Australia
83 Alexander Street,
Crows Nest NSW 2065
Phone: +61 (0)2 8425 0100
murdochbooks.com.au
info@murdochbooks.com.au

Murdoch Books UK
Ormond House,
26–27 Boswell Street,
London WC1N 3JZ
Phone: +44 (0) 20 8785 5995
murdochbooks.co.uk
info@murdochbooks.co.uk

For corporate orders and custom publishing contact our business
development team at salesenquiries@murdochbooks.com.au

Publisher: Corinne Roberts
Editorial Manager: Jane Price
Design Manager: Madeleine Kane
Editor: Kim Rowney
Photographer: Armelle Habib
Stylist: Deborah Kaloper
Production Manager: Rachel Walsh

ISBN 978 1 74336 840 4 Australia
ISBN 978 1 74336 841 1 UK
A cataloguing-in-publication entry is available from the catalogue of the
National Library of Australia at nla.gov.au
A catalogue record for this book is available from the British Library

Colour reproduction by Splitting Image Colour Studio Pty Ltd, Clayton, Victoria
Printed by Hang Tai Printing Company Ltd, China

MEASURES GUIDE: We have used 20 ml (4 teaspoon) tablespoon measures.
If you are using a 15 ml (3 teaspoon) tablespoon add an extra teaspoon of
the ingredient for each tablespoon specified.

IMPORTANT: Those who might be at risk from the effects of salmonella poisoning
(the elderly, pregnant women, young children and those suffering from immune
deficiency diseases) should consult their doctor with any concerns about eating
raw or lightly cooked eggs.